The Pocket Book
of Prayers

EDITED BY JIM PALMER

W PUBLISHING GROUP
A Division of Thomas Nelson Publishers
Since 1798
www.wpublishinggroup.com

Published by W Publishing Group, a Division of Thomas Nelson, Inc., P.O. Box
141000, Nashville, Tennessee, 37214.

W Publishing Group books may be purchased in bulk for educational, business,
fundraising, or sales promotional use. For information, please email
SpecialMarkets@ThomasNelson.com.

All Scripture quotations, unless otherwise indicated, are taken from The King
James Version of the Bible (KJV).

Other Scripture references are from the following sources:
    The Holy Bible, New Century Version (NCV), copyright © 1987, 1988, 1991
    by Word Publishing, a division of Thomas Nelson, Inc. Used by permission.

    Holy Bible, New Living Translation (NLT), copyright © 1996. Used by per-
    mission of Tyndale House Publishers, Inc., Wheaton, Illinois 60189. All
    rights reserved.

Editorial Staff: Shady Oaks Studio, Bedford, Texas
Cover Design: Kirk DouPonce, DogEared Design.com

Library of Congress Cataloging-in-Publication Data
The pocket book of prayers / edited by Jim Palmer.
    p. cm.
Summary: "Compilation of prayers said by noted believers in God throughout
history"—Provided by publisher.
ISBN 0-8499-0505-2 (tradepaper)
1. Prayers.   I. Palmer, Jim, 1964–
BV245.P63   2005
242'.8—dc22   2005003204

Printed in Peru
05 06 07 08 09 QW 9 8 7 6 5 4 3 2 1

The Pocket Book

of *Prayers*

For Pam and Jessica

With special thanks to
the Pilgrimage Project

Introduction

Prayer is conversation with God.
—Saint Clement of Rome, AD 90

There is a river that runs so true through the epic story of God's redemption of the world. It is the enduring conversation between God and man—a river of prayer. One can locate the mouth of this river at the dawn of civilization where the ancient Old Testament scriptures describe *Elohim* creating the primal parents of the human race. Out of the dust of the earth God fashioned them, filled their lungs with the breath of life, and bid them to a relationship with himself. The conversation began.

You can follow the river through the ages and across the continents through biblical records, Celtic oral traditions, monastic liturgies, spirituals and hymns, private journals and personal letters, and cathedral inscriptions. Follow the river of prayer long enough and inevitably you will find yourself eavesdropping upon the intimate reflections of some of history's most pivotal people in situations that would shape their times.

The river winds along the rocky coasts of Ireland, where Saint Patrick boldly called upon God's protection around the Ebenezer Baptist Church in Atlanta, where Martin Luther King Jr. wrestled with God over the suffering of the civil-rights movement, through the villages of Calcutta, where

Mother Teresa pleaded for divine assistance in caring for the needs of orphans; and along ground zero in New York City, where a young mother stands with twins in tow seeking the strength of God to carry on. It also runs alongside the spiritual pilgrimage of countless souls who sought to know, love, and follow God and who discovered deep delight in the knowing and loving and following.

Though simply reflecting upon the Christian prayers in this spiritual anthology will inspire, I most hope they will compel you to start, to begin anew, or to remain faithful in your own conversation with God. Throughout the ages, men and women have stood in the river by utilizing the prayers of others to give expression to their own heart before God. Whether it is seeking guidance amid confusion, courage in the face of fear, healing from heartache, hope and peace in circumstances of despair, or a desire to know and experience God more deeply in your life, consider this book of prayers a sacred pathway for your daily journey of speaking and listening to God.

In addition to the prayers themselves, this compilation is a treasure chest of spiritual wisdom about prayer, including intermittent quotes from devoted followers of Christ throughout history. The book can be a helpful spiritual companion for you personally and useful in many ways for groups seeking to grow in prayer. May the eyes of your soul be enlightened to the unfailing love of God for you, and may your life be set ablaze with love for God.

*P*ray
without
ceasing.

—1 THESSALONIANS 5:17

*D*ay by day, dear Lord, of Thee

three things I pray:

To see Thee more clearly,

To love Thee more dearly,

To follow Thee more nearly.

—RICHARD OF CHICESTER

*B*e thou a bright flame

before me,

Be thou a guiding star

above me,

Be thou a smooth path

before me,

Be thou a kindly shepherd

behind me,

Today—tonight—and forever.

—SAINT COLUMBA

$\mathcal{E}$ternal God, you have been the hope and joy of many generations, and who in all ages has given men the power to seek you and in seeking you to find you, grant me, I pray you, a clearer vision of your truth, a greater faith in your power, and a more confident assurance of your love.

—JOHN BAILLIE

Lord Jesus Christ,

Son of God and son of Mary,

You are the radiant start of the morning.

Come and deliver us from our fears

And the darkness in our everyday lives.

As the Church in earlier times

Once cried for you,

We cry again with one voice:

Come, Lord Jesus, come!

Look with mercy upon us

Who await your coming,

And make shine on us

Your saving light.

—BYZANTINE PRAYER

*Y*ield room for some little time to God; and rest for a little time in him. Enter the inner chamber of your mind; shut out all thoughts except that of God, and such as can help you in seeking him; close your door and seek him. Speak now, my whole heart! Speak now to God; saying, I seek your face; your face, Lord will I seek. And come now, Lord my God, teach my heart where and how it may seek you, where and how it may find you.

——SAINT ANSELM

O God,

when in Jesus you walked this earth,

you had no place to call your own,

no place to lay your head.

As we stand by the

landless and the homeless

and support those who

struggle alongside them,

may we stand by you,

seeing your face and image there.

—BARBARA VALLACOTT

From the cowardice that

dare not face new truth

From the laziness that is contented

with half truth

From the arrogance that thinks it

knows all truth,

Good Lord, deliver me.

—KENYAN PRAYER

O Come, O Holy Spirit, come!
Come as holy fire and burn in us,
Come as holy wind and cleanse us,
Come as holy light and lead us,
Come as holy truth and teach us,
Come as holy forgiveness and
   free us,
Come as holy love and enfold us,
Come as holy power and enable us,
Come as holy life and dwell in us.
Convict us, convert us,
Consecrate us, until we are
   wholly thine.

—ANCIENT COLLECT

I rise today with the power of God
  to guide me,
the might of God to uphold me,
the wisdom of God to teach me,
the eye of God to watch over me,
the ear of God to hear me,
the word of God to give me speech,
the hand of God to protect me,
the path of God to lie before me,
the shield of God to shelter me,
the host of God to defend me
  against the snares of the devil and
  the temptations of the world,
against every man who mediates injury
  to me,
whether far or near.

—BREASTPLATE OF SAINT PATRICK

The Lord taught us to pray

not only in words,

but also in actions.

—SAINT CYPRIAN

OF CARTHAGE

Be Thou my Vision, O Lord of my heart;
Nought be all else to me, save that Thou art—
Thou my best thought, by day or by night,
Waking or sleeping, Thy presence my light.

Riches I heed not, nor man's empty praise,
Thou mine inheritance, now and always:
Thou and Thou only, first in my heart,
High King of heaven, my Treasure Thou art.

High King of heaven, my victory won,
May I reach heaven's joys, O bright heaven's Sun!
Heart of my own heart, whatever befall,
Still be my Vision, O Ruler of all.

—MARY BYRNE

*L*ord of the excluded,

Open my ears to those

I would prefer not to hear,

Open my life to those

I would prefer not to know,

Open my heart to those

I would prefer not to love,

And so open my eyes to see

Where I exclude You.

—IONA ABBEY PRAYER

*L*ord, let your glory be my goal, your

word my rule, and

then your will be done.

—Charles I

$\mathcal{O}$ God, our father, by whose mercy and
might the world turns safely into darkness
and returns again into light: we give into
your hands our unfinished tasks, our unre-
solved problems, and our unfulfilled hopes,
knowing that only that which you bless will
prosper. To your great love and protection
we commit each other and all your people,
knowing that you alone are our sure
defender, through Jesus Christ, our Lord.

—SOUTH INDIA PRAYER

*C*ome, Holy Spirit

Bend what is rigid in me,

Melt what is frozen.

—GREGORIAN CHANT

*S*ince the practice of virtue and the observance
of the commandments form part of prayer, those
who pray well as work at their tasks they have to
do, and combine their prayer with a suitable activity, will be "praying always." This is the only way
in which it is
possible never to stop praying.

—Origen of Alexandria

$\mathcal{P}$rayer is the
central avenue
God uses to
transform us.

—RICHARD J. FOSTER

*L*et me seek you in my desire,

Let me desire you in my seeking.

Let me find you by loving you,

Let me love you when I find you.

—SAINT ANSELM

Here is a gaping sore, Lord;

   half the world diets,

      the other half hungers;

   half the world is housed,

      the other half homeless;

   half the world pursues profit,

      the other half senses loss.

Redeem our souls,

redeem our peoples,

redeem our times.

—JOHN BELL

ℳay the light of God

illumine the heart of my soul.

May the flame of Christ

kindle me to love.

May the fire of the Spirit

free me to live

this day, tonight and forever.

—CELTIC BENEDICTION

*L*ord, make me an instrument of Your peace.

    Where there is hatred, let me sow love;

    Where there is injury, pardon;

    Where there is doubt, faith;

    Where there is despair, hope;

    Where there is darkness, light;

    Where there is sadness, joy.

O Divine Master, grant that I may not so much seek to be consoled as to console, to be understood as to understand, to be loved as to love. For it is in giving that we receive; it is in pardoning that we are pardoned; it is in dying that we are born to eternal life.

—SAINT FRANCIS OF ASSISI

*A*lmighty God, we commend to your gracious care and keeping all the men and women of our armed forces at home and abroad. Defend them day by day with your heavenly grace; strengthen them in their trials and temptations; give them courage to face the perils which beset them; and grant them a sense of your abiding presence wherever they may be; through Jesus Christ our Lord. Amen.

—BOOK OF COMMON PRAYER

Lord Jesus Christ,

Son of God,

have mercy upon me.

—THE JESUS PRAYER

*I*n a single day I have

prayed as many as

a hundred times,

and in the night

almost as often.

—SAINT PATRICK

*F*ather, it is a humbling thing to be died for. On this day let me remember that Jesus Christ, your Son, did exactly that for me. And he went to his death knowing full well how often I would forget his love. Let no pride keep me from kneeling at the foot of that cross. In the name of Jesus my Savior I pray. Amen.

—PETER MARSHALL

*L*ong is our winter,

Dark is our night;

Come, set us free,

O Saving Light!

—GERMAN PRAYER

*G*od be in my head,

and in my understanding;

God be in my eyes,

and in my looking;

God be in my mouth,

and in my speaking;

God be in my heart,

and in my thinking;

God be at my end

and at my departing. Amen.

—OLD SARUM PRIMER

Watch, dear Lord, with those who wake, or watch, or weep tonight, and give your angels charge over those who sleep. Tend your sick ones, O Lord Christ. Rest your weary ones. Bless your dying ones. Soothe your suffering ones. Pity your afflicted ones. Shield your joyous ones. And all, for your love's sake. Amen.

—SAINT AUGUSTINE

*I*n the busyness of this day
grant me a stillness of seeing, O God.
In the conflicting voices of my heart
grant me a calmness of hearing.
Let my seeing and my hearing
my words and my actions
be rooted in a silent certainty of your
presence.
Let my passions for life
and the longings for justice that stir
within me
be grounded in the experience
of your stillness.
Let my life be rooted in the ground
of your peace, O God,
let me be rooted in the depths
of your peace.

—CELTIC MORNING PRAYER

O Lord,

you have given us your word

for a light

to shine upon our path;

grant us to so meditate on that word,

and to follow its teaching,

that we may find in it the light

that shines

more and more until that perfect day;

through Jesus Christ our Lord.

—JEROME

*I*f God is slow in
answering your request,
and you ask
but do not promptly receive
anything, do not be upset,
for you are not wiser
than God.

—ABRAHAM OF NATHPAR

*O*ur Father in heaven,

Hallowed be Your name.

Your kingdom come,

Your will be done

On earth as it is in heaven.

Give us this day our daily bread.

And forgive us our debts,

As we forgive our debtors.

And do not lead us into temptation,

But deliver us from the evil one.

For Yours is the kingdom

And the power

And the glory forever.

—THE LORD'S PRAYER

*A*lmighty God,

heavenly Father, you have blessed us with

the joy and care of children. Give us calm

strength and patient wisdom as we bring

them up, that we may teach them to love

whatever is just and true and good, follow-

ing the example of our Savior Jesus Christ.

Amen.

—BOOK OF COMMON PRAYER

*G*lory be to God the Father,

God the Son,

and God the Holy Spirit.

As it was in the beginning,

so it is now and so it shall ever be,

world without end.

Alleluia. Amen.

—THE GLORIA

*Y*ou, O Eternal Trinity, are a deep sea into which, the more I enter, the more I find, and the more I find, the more I seek. O abyss, O eternal Godhead, O sea profound, what more could you give me than yourself?

—SAINT CATHERINE OF SIENA

O Lord, who art as the Shadow of a great Rock in a weary land, who beholdest thy weak creatures weary of labor, weary of pleasure, weary of hope deferred, weary of self; in thine abundant compassion, and unutterable tenderness, bring us, I pray thee, unto thy rest.

—CHRISTINA ROSSETTI

*I*f you really wish to achieve

spiritual stillness and to guard your

heart successfully, then let the prayer

"Lord Jesus, have mercy upon me"

become one with your breathing, and

in a few days you will see how it can

all be achieved.

—HESYCHIOS

*C*ome, my Light, and illumine my darkness. Come, my Life, and revive me from death. Come, my Physician, and heal my wounds. Come, Flame of divine love, and burn up the thorns of my sins, kindling my heart with the flame of your love. Come, my King, sit upon the throne of my heart and reign there. For you alone are my King and my Lord.

—SAINT DIMITRII OF ROSTOV

God grant me the serenity to accept

the things I cannot change;

courage to change the things I can;

and wisdom to know the difference.

—REINHOLD NIEBUHR

*Y*ou have made us one with Your saints in heaven and earth. Grant that in our pilgrimage, we may always be supported by this fellowship of love and prayer, and know ourselves to be surrounded by their witness to Your power and mercy. Amen.

—COLLECT FOR THE COMMUNITY OF SAINTS

May your peace

shine among us

and your love set us free,

Lord, we pray.

Keep us persevering in faith

and set in our hearts

the desire for your Kingdom.

—Taize Prayer

*D*ear Lord Jesus Christ, my longing is so great that I cannot express it in words. I know not how to ask. See my heart. What more shall I say? My suffering is greater than all my complaining. I cannot counsel myself with reason nor comfort myself with my own courage. Comfortless, helpless, and forsaken, I am completely at loss. My God, you will not abandon my hope. You will hear my prayer and satisfy my desires. I will pray and wait for your grace. Hear me and fulfill my hope. Amen.

—MARTIN LUTHER

*S*overeign Father, help me to remember that no problem is too small to escape Your concern and no
perplexity is too great to resist Your solutions. I know You will go before me to show me the way, behind me to press me forward, beside me to give me courage, above me to protect me, and within me to give me wisdom and
discernment.

—LLOYD JOHN OGILVIE

Most merciful God, we confess that we have sinned against you in thought, word, and deed, by what we have done, and by what we have left undone. We have not loved you with our whole heart; we have not loved our neighbors as ourselves. We are truly sorry and we humbly repent. For the sake of your Son Jesus Christ, have mercy on us and forgive us; that we may delight in your will, and walk in your ways, to the glory of your Name. Amen.

—BOOK OF COMMON PRAYER

*A*nyone is capable of a very close and intimate dialogue with the Lord. It is true, some find it easier than others. But remember, the Lord knows this fact, too! So begin. Whether you are one who finds this easy or difficult is not important. Begin. He knows which category you are in! It just may be that He is only waiting for a resolution on your part to start. So make this resolution. Now!

—BROTHER LAWRENCE

The LORD is my shepherd; I shall not want. He makes me to lie down in green pastures; He leads me beside the still waters. He restores my soul; He leads me in the paths of righteousness for His name's sake. Yea, though I walk through the valley of the shadow of death, I will fear no evil; for You are with me; Your rod and Your staff, they comfort me. You prepare a table before me in the presence of my enemies; You anoint my head with oil; my cup runs over. Surely goodness and mercy shall follow me all the days of my life; and I will dwell in the house of the LORD forever.

—KING DAVID
PSALM 23

*I*n the beginning, O God,

your Spirit swept over the chaotic deep

like a wild wind and creation was born.

In the turbulence of my own life and the

unsettled waters of the world today let

there be new birthings of

   your Spirit.

In the currents of my own heart and the

upheavals of the world today

let there be new birthings of your

   mighty Spirit.

—CELTIC MORNING PRAYER

*T*hank you

for unlocking doors we cannot open.

Thank you

for locking doors we cannot lock.

Thank you

for being the key.

Thank you

for giving us YOURSELF!

—PETER LORD

Show me today, O Lord,

that one to whom I am

to give a cup of cold water

in your name.

—F. B. MEYER

*M*y Father, you call me out to freedom. And I long to live confident and at liberty in you—not bound by all the things that hold me. Now I hear you coming for me . . . turning the key . . . and I hear your voice calling to my soul, saying "Rise, and begin to walk with me to a new place." Today, I commit myself to a journey that will lead me deeper into your love.

—SAINT JOHN OF THE CROSS

May the LORD bless you

and protect you.

May the LORD smile on you

and be gracious to you.

May the LORD show you his favor

and give you his peace.

—MOSES

NUMBERS 6:24–26 (NLT)

*T*he best prayers

have often more

groans than words.

—JOHN BUNYAN

God to enfold me,
God to surround me,
God in my speaking,
God in my thinking.

God in my sleeping,
God in my waking,
God in my watching,
God in my hoping.

God in my life,
God in my lips,
God in my soul,
God in my heart.

—GAELIC GRACE

*L*ord, bestow on me two gifts,

to forget myself

never to forget thee.

Keep me from self-love, self-pity, self-will

in every guise and disguise.

nor ever let me measure myself by

myself.

Save me from self,

My tempter, seducer, jailor;

corrupting desire at the spring,

closing the avenues of grace,

leading me down the streets of death.

Rather, let my soul devote to thee

its aspirations, affections, resolutions.

—ERIC MILNER-WHITE

*D*ear Lord,

So far today I've done all right . . .

I haven't gossiped, lost my temper,

been greedy, grumpy, nasty,

selfish or over-indulgent.

I'm very thankful for that.

But in a few minutes, Lord,

I'm going to get out of bed,

and from then on,

I'm going to need a lot of help.

—AUTHOR UNKNOWN

*B*e present, most merciful God, and
protect us through the silent hours of this
night, so that we who are wearied by the
changes and chances of this world, may
take rest in your abiding changelessness.
Through Christ our Lord. Amen.

—AMBROSE OF MILAN

Teach me, O Lord, the way of Your statutes, and I shall keep it to the end. Give me understanding, and I shall keep Your law, Indeed, I shall observe it with my whole heart. Make me walk in the path of Your commandments, for I delight in it. Incline my heart to Your testimonies, and not to covetousness. Turn away my eyes from looking at worthless things, and revive me in Your way.

—PSALM 119:33–37

Almighty God, in giving us dominion over things on earth, you made us fellow workers in your creation. Give us wisdom and reverence so to use the resources of nature, that no one may suffer from our abuse of them, and that generations yet to come may continue to praise you for your bounty, through Jesus Christ our Lord. Amen.

—BOOK OF COMMON PRAYER

*I*n your life
of prayer and
meditation, seek the
command that God
addresses to you and
put it into practice
without delay.

—THE RULE OF TAIZE

*T*he vitality of God be mine this day

the vitality of the God of life.

The passion of Christ be mine this day

the passion of the Christ of love.

The wakefulness of the Spirit be mine this day

the wakefulness of the Spirit of justice.

The vitality and passion and wakefulness

of God be mine that

I may be fully alive this day.

The vitality and passion and wakefulness

　of God

that I may be fully alive.

—CELTIC PRAYER

Almighty God, thank Thee for the job of this day. May we find gladness in all its toil and difficulty, its pleasure and success, and even in its failure and sorrow. We would look always away from ourselves, and behold the glory and the need of the world that we may have the will and the strength to bring the gift of gladness to others; that with them we stand to bear the burden and heat of the day and offer Thee the praise of work well done. Amen.

—BISHOP CHARLES LEWIS SLATTERY

𝒟ear Lord, thank You for this day.
Hold my hand and give me courage to
carry the cross You have chosen for me.
Let me never complain. Let me smile and
give strength to my family and friends
and to all I come in contact with. I accept
what I have and will not ask, "Why me?"
I will fight until You take me because it is
my belief that I was made to serve You
on earth—and death is my final reward.

—BETTY MCELWEE

Father, I abandon myself into your hands, do with me what you will. Whatever you may do, I thank you. I am ready for all, I accept all. Let only your will be done in me and in all your creatures—I wish no more than this, O Lord. Into your hands I commend my soul, I offer it to you with all the love of my heart, for I love you Lord, and so need to give myself, to surrender myself into your hands, without reserve, and with boundless confidence, For you are my Father.

—CHARLES DE FOUCAULD

*M*ay God have mercy on us,

and bless us.

May He make the light of His face

shine on us,

and may He have mercy on us,

that we may know His way on earth

and His salvation

in all the nations.

—MEDIEVAL PRYMER

*P*lough deep in me, great Lord, heavenly husbandman, that my being may be a tilled field, the roots of grace spreading far and wide, until Thou alone art seen in me, Thy beauty golden like summer harvest, Thy fruitfulness as autumn plenty.

—PURITAN PRAYER

*ℬ*eloved, to Thee I raise my whole being, a vessel emptied of self. Accept, O Lord, this my emptiness, and so fill me with Thy Self—Thy Light, Thy Love, Thy Life—that these Thy precious Gifts may radiate through me and overflow the chalice of my heart into the hearts of all with whom I come in contact this day, revealing unto them the beauty of Thy joy and Wholeness and the serenity of Thy Peace which nothing can destroy.

—FRANCIS NUTTALL

The most precious privilege in talking with Christ is this intimacy which we can have with Him.

—BROTHER LAWRENCE

*C*ircle me, Lord.
Keep protection near
and danger afar.

Circle me, Lord.
Keep hope within.
Keep doubt without.

Circle me, Lord.
Keep light near
and darkness afar.

Circle me, Lord.
Keep peace within.
Keep evil out.

—DAVID ADAM

Disturb us, Lord, when
We are too well pleased with ourselves,
When our dreams have come true
Because we have dreamed too little,
When we arrived safely
Because we sailed too close to shore.

Disturb us, Lord, to dare more boldly,
To venture on wider seas
Where storms will show your mastery;
Where losing sight of land,
We shall find the stars.

We ask you to push back
The horizons of our hopes;
And to push into the future
In strength, courage, hope, and love.

—SIR FRANCIS DRAKE

$\mathcal{A}$nd now, O God, give me a quiet mind, as I lie down to rest. Dwell in my thoughts until sleep overtake me. Let me not be fretted by any anxiety over the lesser interests of life. Let no troubled dreams disturb me, so that I may awake refreshed and ready for the tasks of another day.

—JOHN BAILLIE

*Y*ou wonderfully created,

Almighty God,

and yet more wonderfully restored the

dignity of our human nature:

Grant that we who remember the story of

the One You sent,

the One Who humbled Himself to

share in our humanity,

may come to share in His divine life.

Amen.

—COLLECT FOR THE SEASONS

I take God the Father to be my God;

I take God the Son to be my Savior;

I take the Holy Spirit to be my Sanctifier;

I take the Word of God to be my rule;

I take the people of God to be my people;

And I do hereby dedicate and yield my

    whole self to the Lord;

And I do this deliberately, freely, and

    forever.

Amen.

—MATTHEW HENRY

Breathe on me, Breath of God,

Fill me with life anew,

That I may love what

Thou dost love,

And do what Thou wouldst do.

—EDWIN HATCH

O God, we pray for all those in the
world who are suffering from injustice:
For those who are discriminated against
because of their race, color or religion; for
those imprisoned for working for the relief
of oppression; for those who are hounded
for speaking the inconvenient truth; for
those tempted to violence as a cry against
overwhelming hardship; for those
deprived of reasonable health and education; for those suffering from hunger and
famine; for those too weak to help them-

selves and who have no one else to help them; for the unemployed who cry out for work but do not find it. We pray for anyone of our acquaintance who is personally affected by injustice. Forgive us, Lord, if we unwittingly share in the conditions or in a system that perpetuates injustice. Show us how we can serve children and make your love practical by washing their feet.

—MOTHER TERESA

*E*verything that one
turns in the direction
of God is a prayer.

—SAINT IGNATIUS LOYOLA

O Love, that wilt not let me go,

I rest my weary soul in Thee;

I give Thee back the life I owe,

That in Thine ocean depths its flow

May richer, fuller be.

—GEORGE MATHESON

*A*s the mother understands

the wordless child,

the wise teacher hears

the stammering boy,

the sage hears the

awe-silenced pilgrim,

hear us, our Father,

as we hold up to thee

our longings and our need.

In Christ's name. Amen.

—EDWARD TYLER

*O*h, the depth of the riches both of the wisdom and the knowledge of God! How unsearchable are His judgments and His ways past finding out! For who has known the mind of the LORD? Or who has become His counselor? Or who has first given to Him, and it shall be repaid to him? For of Him and through Him and to Him are all things, to whom be glory forever. Amen.

—SAINT PAUL
ROMANS 11:33–36

*G*ive us, O Lord, a steadfast heart, which no unworthy affection may drag downwards; give us an unconquered heart, which no tribulation can wear out; give us an upright heart, which no unworthy purpose may tempt aside. Bestow upon us also, O Lord our God, understanding to know you, diligence to seek you, wisdom to find you and a faithfulness that may finally embrace you, through Jesus Christ our Lord.

—SAINT THOMAS AQUINAS

God of your goodness,

give me yourself,

for you are sufficient for me . . .

If I were to ask anything less

I should always be in want,

for in you alone do I have all.

—JULIAN OF NORWICH

*F*orgive us, O Christ, for all our wanderings. Forgive us for not listening to your voice calling us into right ways. Forgive us for our complaining and our worrying that have made us lose trust in you. Forgive us for anger and selfishness and for greed. For all these we are sorry and pray that they may be taken from us.

—A. MURRAY SMITH

S et our hearts on fire with love for
you, O Christ our God, that in its flame
we may love you with all our heart, with
all our mind, with all our soul and with all
our strength and our neighbors as ourselves, so that, keeping your commandments, we may glorify you, the giver of all
good gifts.

—EASTERN ORTHODOX CHURCH

*A*s our tropical sun gives forth light, so let the rays from your face enter every nook of my being and drive away all darkness within.

—PHILIPPINE PRAYER

*I*t is an old custom of the servants of God to have some little prayer ready and to be frequently darting them up to Heaven during the day, lifting their minds to God out of the mire of the world. He who adopts this plan will get great fruits with little pains.

—PHILIP NERI

*F*ather,

I am seeking.

I am hesitant and uncertain,

but will you, O God,

watch over every step of mine

and guide me?

—SAINT AUGUSTINE

*G*rant me, O Lord, to know what is worth knowing, to love what is worth loving, to praise what delights you most, to value what is precious in your sight, to hate what is offensive to you. Do not let me judge by what I see, nor pass sentence according to what I hear, but to judge rightly between things that differ and above all to search out and do what pleases you, through Jesus Christ our Lord.

—THOMAS À KEMPIS

I pray that Christ will live in your hearts by faith and that your life will be strong in love and be built on love. And I pray that you and all God's holy people will have the power to understand the greatness of Christ's love—how wide and how long and how high and how deep that love is. Christ's love is greater than anyone can ever know, but I pray that you will be able to know that love. Then you can be filled with the fullness of God. With God's power working in us, God can do much, much more than anything we can ask or imagine. To him be glory in the church and in Christ Jesus, forever and ever. Amen.

—SAINT PAUL

EPHESIANS 3:17–21 (NCV)

Thank you, Lord Jesus,
that you will be our hiding place
whatever happens.

—CORRIE TEN BOOM

*L*ord, here is my Bible,

here is this quiet room,

here is this quiet time,

and here am I.

Open my eyes; open my mind;

open my heart;

and speak.

—DICK WILLIAMS

O heavenly Father, in whom we live and move and have our being, we humbly pray you so to guide and govern us by the Holy Spirit that in all the cares and occupations of our daily life we may never forget you, but remember that we are ever walking in your sight; for your own name's sake.

—ANCIENT COLLECT

*S*peak, Lord,

for your servant hears.

Grant us ears to hear,

Eyes to see,

Wills to obey,

Hearts to love;

Then declare what you will,

Reveal what you will,

Command what you will,

Demand what you will.

—CHRISTINA ROSSETTI

Lord Jesus, I don't know much

about you,

But I am willing to learn;

And I am ready to give all that I know

of myself

To all that I know of you;

And I am willing to go on learning.

—DONALD COGGAN

*T*o clasp the hands in prayer is the beginning of an uprising against the disorder of the world.

—KARL BARTH

*G*ive me a candle of the Spirit, O God, as I go down into the deeps of my being. Show me the hidden things, the creatures of my dreams, the storehouse of forgotten memories and hurts. Take me down to the spring of my life and tell me my nature and my name. Give me freedom to grow, so that I may become that self, the seed of which you planted in me at my making. Out of the deeps I cry to you, O God.

—GEORGE APPLETON

*Y*ou are the place of all things calm

You are the place to hide from harm

You are the light that shines in dark

You are the heart's eternal spark

You are the door that's open wide

You are the guest who waits inside

You are the stranger at the door

You are the calling of the poor

You are my Lord and with me still

You are my love, keep me from ill

You are the light, the truth, the way

You are my Savior this very day.

—CELTIC ORAL TRADITION

*E*ternal God, who hast set before us life and death for our choice, and hast given us Jesus Christ to be the way, the truth, and the life; help us to enter that way, to receive that truth, and to live by that life. Suffer us not to miss the purpose of our creation, but make us to be sons and daughters of thine and servants of thy kingdom. Through the same Jesus Christ our Lord

—DONALD BAILLIE

*J*ust as day declines to evening, so often
after some little pleasure my heart declines
into depression. Everything seems dull, every
action feels like a burden. If anyone speaks, I
scarcely listen. If anyone knocks, I scarcely
hear. My heart is as hard as flint. Then I go
out into the field to meditate, to read the holy
Scriptures, and I write down my deepest
thoughts in a letter to you. And suddenly,
your grace, dear Jesus, shatters the darkness
with daylight, lifts the burden, relieves the ten-
sion. Soon tears follow sighs, and heavenly joy
floods over me with tears.

—AELRED OF RIEVAULX

*E*ternal God,

the refuge of all your children,

in our weakness

you are our strength,

in our darkness our light,

in our sorrow our comfort and peace.

May we always live in your presence,

and serve you in our daily lives;

through Jesus Christ our Lord.

—BONIFACE

For the beauty of the earth,
For the beauty of the skies,
For the love which from our birth
Over and around us lies:
Lord of all, to Thee we raise
This our hymn of grateful praise.

For the beauty of each hour
Of the day and of the night,
Hill and vale and tree and flower,
Sun and moon and stars of light:
Lord of all, to Thee we raise
This our hymn of grateful praise.

—F. S. PIERPOINT

*M*y spirit longs for Thee
Within my troubled breast,
Though I unworthy be
Of so divine a guest.

Of so divine a guest
Unworthy though I be,
Yet has my heart no rest
Unless it comes from thee.

Amazing grace! How sweet the sound
That saved a wretch like me;
I once was lost, but now am found;
Was blind, but now I see.

—JOHN NEWTON

𝒲rite your blessed name, O Lord, upon my heart, there to remain so indelibly engraved, that no prosperity, no adversity shall ever move me from your love. Be to me a strong tower of defense, a comforter in tribulation, a deliverer in distress, a very present help in trouble and a guide to heaven through the many temptations and dangers of this life.

—THOMAS À KEMPIS

The more you pray,

the easier it becomes.

The easier it becomes,

the more you'll pray.

—MOTHER TERESA

*L*ord Jesus Christ, you said that you are the Way, the Truth, and the Life. Help us not to stray from you, for you are the Way; nor to distrust you, for you are the Truth; nor to rest on any other than you, as you are the Life. You have taught us what to believe, what to do, what to hope, and where to take our rest. Give us grace to follow you, the Way, to learn from you, the Truth, and to live in you, the Life.

—DESIDERIUS ERASMUS

*L*ord Jesus, make yourself to me

A living, bright reality.

More present to faith's vision keen

Than any outward object seen.

—HUDSON TAYLOR

The Sacred Three

My fortress be

Encircling me

Come and be round

My hearth, my home.

—TRADITIONAL
HEBRIDEAN CHANT

*F*ather,

give us wisdom to perceive you,

intellect to understand you,

diligence to seek you,

patience to wait for you,

eyes to behold you,

a heart to meditate on you

and a life to proclaim you,

through the power of the Spirit

of our Lord Jesus Christ.

—SAINT BENEDICT

$\mathcal{G}$rant to your servants, O God,

to be set on fire with your love,

to be strengthened by your power,

to be illuminated by your Spirit,

to be filled with your grace,

and to go forward by your help;

through Jesus Christ our Lord.

—GALLICAN SACRAMENTARY

𝒪 Lord, convert the world—and

begin with me.

—CHINESE STUDENT'S PRAYER

*F*or those who truly desire
a life of prayer the only way
to achieve it is by praying.

—MOTHER MARY CLARE

*S*trengthen us, O God, to relieve the oppressed, to hear the groans of poor prisoners, to reform the abuses of all professions; that many be made not poor to make a few rich, for Jesus Christ's sake.

—OLIVER CROMWELL

*M*ay your Spirit guide my mind,

Which is so often dull and empty.

Let my thoughts be always on you,

And let me see you in all things.

May your Spirit quicken my soul,

Which is so often listless and lethargic.

Let my soul be awake to your presence,

And let me know you in all things.

May your Spirit melt my heart,

Which is so often cold and indifferent.

Let my heart be warmed by your love,

And let me feel you in all things.

—JOHANN A. FREYLINGHAUSEN

*L*ord, make me see thy glory

in every place.

—MICHELANGELO

*M*y Lord and my God,

take me from all that

keeps me from thee.

My Lord and my God,

grant me all that leads me to thee.

My Lord and my God,

take me from myself and

give me completely to thee.

—NICHOLAS OF FLUE

*L*ord, come to me,

my door is open.

—MICHEL QUOIST

O God, early in the morning I cry to you. Help me pray and to concentrate my thoughts on you; I cannot do this alone. In me there is darkness, but with you there is light; I am lonely, but you do not leave me; I am feeble in heart, but with you there is help; I am restless, but with you there is peace. In me there is bitterness, but with you there is patience; I do not understand your ways, but you know the way for me.

—DIETRICH BONHOEFFER

I praise thee for the life that stirs
within me; I praise thee for the bright and
beautiful world into which I go;
I praise thee for earth and sea and sky, for
scudding cloud and singing bird; I praise
thee for the work thou hast given me to
do; I praise thee for all that thou has given
me to fill my leisure hours; I praise thee
for my friends; I praise thee for music and
books and good company and all pure
pleasures.

—JOHN BAILLIE

*G*rant, O Lord, that your love may so

fill our lives that we may count

nothing too small to do for you, nothing

too much to give you, and nothing too

hard to bear, for Jesus Christ's sake.

—SAINT IGNATIUS OF LOYOLA

The man who prays
will have a heart as wide
as the love of God itself.

—SAINT CLARE OF ASSISI

Restore the homes deprived of joy,

Deliver those in pain,

Bring justice, liberty from fear,

And hope to live again.

—ANNA BRIGGS

In the darkness of the evening the eyes of my heart are awake to you. In the quiet of the night I long to hear again intimations of your love. In the sufferings of the world and the struggles of my life I seek your graces of healing. At the heart of the brokenness around me and in the hidden depths of my own soul I seek your touch of healing, O God, for there you reside. In the hidden depths of life, O God, there you reside.

—CELTIC PRAYER

*G*od of eternal life, bless all who contemplate taking their own life. Grant them peace from the internal fears and doubts, from the turmoil of failures, from the pain and suffering in their souls. Endow them with hope for the days ahead, courage to make new beginnings, and love to strengthen their resolve to live; in the name of Christ we pray.

—VIENNA COBB ANDERSON

O Lord Jesus

Please abide with me

Dispel my deep loneliness!

No one can be my companion forever

But you are the Lord who is everywhere,

Present at all times.

Only you are my dear companion and savior.

In the long dark night,

Among the silent shadowy pathways,

I beg you to grasp my hand.

When others have forgotten me,

Please remember me in eternity!

In the name of Jesus.

—ANDREW SONG

*O*pen unto me—light for my darkness.
Open unto me—courage for my fear.
Open unto me—hope for my despair.
Open unto me—peace for my turmoil.
Open unto me—joy for my sorrow.
Open unto me—strength for my weakness.
Open unto me—wisdom for my confusion.
Open unto me—forgiveness for my sins.
Open unto me—tenderness for my thoughts.
Open unto me—love for my hates.
Open unto me—Thy self for my self.
Lord, Lord, open unto me!
Amen.

—HOWARD THURMAN

I was regretting the past and fearing the future. Suddenly God was speaking, "My name is 'I am.'" I waited. God continued, "When you live in the past, with its mistakes and regrets, it is hard. I am not there. My name is not 'I was.' When you live in the future, with its problems and fears, it is hard. I am not there. My name is not 'I will be.' When you live in this moment, it is not hard. I am here. My name is 'I am.'"

—ON KITCHEN WALL OF
SAINT BENEDICT'S MONASTERY

*M*ay there always be work for your
   hands to do
May your purse always hold a coin or two
May the sun always shine upon your
   window pane
May a rainbow be certain to follow each rain
May the hand of a friend always be near you
And may God fill your heart with
   gladness to cheer you.

—AN IRISH BLESSING

*L*ord, I sometimes wander away from you. But this is not because I am deliberately turning my back on you. It is because of the inconstancy of my mind. I weaken in my intention to give my whole soul to you. I fall back into thinking of myself as my own master. But when I wander from you, my life becomes a burden, and within me I find nothing but darkness and wretchedness, fear and anxiety. So I come back to you, and confess that I have sinned against you. And I know you will forgive me.

—Aelred of Rievaulx

*L*ord of My Heart, give me vision to inspire me, that, working or resting, I may always think of You. Lord of My Heart, give me light to guide me, that at home or abroad, I may always walk in Your way. Lord of My Heart, give me wisdom to direct me, that thinking or acting I may always discern right from wrong. Lord of My Heart, give me courage to strengthen me, that, amongst friends or enemies, I may always proclaim Your justice. Lord of My Heart, give me trust to console me, that hungry or well-fed, I may always rely on Your mercy.

—CELTIC ORAL TRADITION

*I*n the rush and noise of life, as you have intervals, step within yourselves and be still. Wait upon God and feel his good presence; this will carry you through your day's business.

—WILLIAM PENN

*J*esus, I wish you would let me wash your feet, since it was by walking around in me that you soiled them. I wish you would give me the task of wiping the stains from your feet, since it was my behavior that put them there. But where can I get the running water I need to wash your feet? If I have no water, at least I have tears. Let me wash your feet with my tears, and wash myself at the same time.

—AMBROSE OF MILAN

*C*ome now, Lord,

and I will be comforted.

Show me your face,

and I shall be saved.

Enter my room,

and I shall be satisfied.

Reveal your beauty,

and my joy will be complete.

—SAINT ANSELM

I need thee every hour, most gracious
   Lord;
No tender voice like thine can peace afford.
I need thee every hour; stay thou near by;
Temptations lose their power when thou
      art nigh.
I need thee every hour, in joy or pain;
Come quickly and abide, or life is vain.
I need thee every hour; teach me thy will;
And thy rich promises in me fulfill.
I need thee, O I need thee,
Every hour I need thee;
O bless me now, my Savior,
I come to Thee!

—ANNIE S. HAWKS

*E*ternal father of my soul,

let my first thought today be of thee, let

my first impulse be to worship thee, let

my first speech be thy name, let my first

action be to kneel before you in prayer.

—JOHN BAILLIE

From this hour my purpose, through thy grace, is to accept and welcome all occurrences, whether pleasing or distasteful to sense, as coming from thy heavenly providence; this shall be my comfort and stay in all my afflictions; in dangers, security, and perfect rest of mind in expectation of future events. Thou alone, O my God, provide, determine, will and choose for me.

—AUGUSTINE BAKER

𝓛ord Jesus Christ, pierce my soul with your love so that I may always long for you alone, who are the bread of angels and fulfillment of the soul's deepest desires. May my heart always hunger and feed on you, so that my soul may be filled with the sweetness of your presence. May my soul thirst for you, who are the source of life, wisdom, knowledge, light and all the riches of God our Father. May I always seek and find you, think about you, speak to you and do everything for the honour and glory of your holy name. Be always my hope, my peace, my refuge and my help in whom my heart is rooted so that I may never be separated from you.

—SAINT BONAVENTURE

*I*f we behave as if we were the only

people for whom life is difficult;

If we believe as if we were far

harder worked than anyone else;

If we behave as if we were the only

people who ever got a raw deal;

If we are far too self-centered and far

too full of self-pity:

Forgive us, O God.

—WILLIAM BARCLAY

*J*esus, how sweet is the very thought of you! You fill my heart with joy. The sweetness of your love surpasses the sweetness of honey. Nothing sweeter than you can be described; no words can express the joy of your love. Only those who have tasted your love for themselves can comprehend it. In your love you listen to all my prayers, even when my wishes are childish, my words confused, and my thoughts foolish. And you answer my prayers, not according to my own misdirected desires, which would bring only bitter misery, but according to my real needs, which brings me sweet joy. Thank you, Jesus, for giving yourself to me.

—BERNARD OF CLAIRVAUX

*I*t becomes essential

that we should endeavor

in prayer to realize the

presence of God.

It may be stated this way:

you have prayed well

if you have spoken to God as

a man speaks to a friend.

—CHARLES SPURGEON

*M*ay thy grace, O Lord, make that possible to me which seems impossible to me by nature.

—AMY CARMICHAEL

*E*ternal Trinity, you are like a deep sea, in which the more I seek, the more I find; and the more I find, the more eagerly I seek.

—SAINT CATHERINE OF SIENA

*G*ive me the insight, Lord, to feel as others feel. Give me the imagination to stand in another's shoes. Your mercy is great because you know in Jesus what it is to be a man. Help me to share in this mercy.

—REX CHAPMAN

Fountain of mercy,

Light of truth,

Faith without limits,

Love without end,

Exemplar of virtue,

Proclaimer of Justice,

Leader of men,

Your footprints show the way to heaven.

—CLEMENT OF ALEXANDRIA

*L*ord, you are here,

Lord, you are there.

You are wherever we go.

Lord, you guide us,

Lord, you protect us.

You are wherever we go.

Lord, we need you,

Lord, we trust you,

You are wherever we go.

Lord, we love you,

Lord, we praise you,

You are wherever we go.

—DINKA DAILY CHANT

*T*each me, my God and King,

In all things thee to see,

And what I do in anything,

To do it as for thee.

—GEORGE HERBERT

*A*h, blessed Lord, I wish I knew

how I might best love you and please you,

and that my love were as sweet to you as

your love is to me.

—MARGERY KEMPE

*W*ho is like you,

Jesus sweet Jesus?

You are the light of

those who are spiritually lost.

You are the life of

those who are spiritually dead.

You are the liberation of

those who are imprisoned by guilt.

You are the glory of those who hate

themselves.

You are the guardian of those who are
paralyzed by fear.

You are the guide of those who are bewil-
dered by falsehood.

You are the peace of
those who are in turmoil.

You are the prince of
those who yearn to be led.

You are the priest of
those who seek the truth.

—JOHANN FREYLINGHAUSEN

*B*uild yourself a cell
in your heart and
retire there to pray.

—SAINT CATHERINE
OF SIENA

𝒪 God, who gives the day for work and the night for sleep, refresh our bodies and our minds through the quiet hours of night, and let our inward eyes be directed towards you, dreaming of your eternal glory.

—LEONINE SACRAMENTARY

O Holy Spirit, As the sun is full of light, the ocean full of water, Heaven full of glory, so may my heart be full of Thee.

—PURITAN PRAYER

*T*he Lord is my rock, my protection,

my Savior. My God is my rock. I can run

to him for safety. He is my shield and my

saving strength, my defender and my

place of safety. . . . In my

trouble I called to the Lord; I cried out to

God. From his temple he heard my voice;

my call for help reached his ears.

—KING DAVID

2 SAMUEL 22:2–3, 7 (NCV)

*L*ord Jesus, make yourself to me

A living, bright reality.

More present to faith's vision keen

Than any outward object seen.

—HUDSON TAYLOR

*T*ake all hate from my heart, O God, and teach me how to take it from the hearts of others. Open my eyes and show me what things in our society make it easy for hatred to flourish and hard for us to conquer it. Then help me to try to change these things. And so open my eyes and my ears that I may this coming day be able to do some work of peace for you.

—ALAN PATON

O what blessedness accompanies devotion, when under all the trials that weary me, the cares that corrode me, the fears that disturb me, the infirmities that oppress me, I can come to Thee in my need and feel peace beyond understanding!

—PURITAN PRAYER

Although within us

there are wounds,

Lord Christ, above all there is

the miracle of your

mysterious presence.

Thus, made lighter or even set free,

we are going with you, the Christ,

from one discovery to another.

—ROGER SCHUTZ

*W*hen you speak,

Jesus hears.

And when Jesus hears,

thunder falls.

And when thunder falls,

the world is changed.

All because someone prayed.

—MAX LUCADO

*B*less all those I know who live alone
from choice, all who live alone following a
death, all who live alone because of estrange-
ment, all who live alone for financial reasons.
Bless each small room I think of, each flat, each
too large old house, wherever one raises her
voice to you in prayer at any time. . . . Single,
married, divorced, young, middle-aged, old—
we are all your children, part of your great
human family. All the time, we need courage
and reassurance and your loving care and presence. Keep us.

—RITA SNOWDEN

O Morning Star, Splendor of Light,

Eternal and Bright Sun of Justice, come

and shine on all who live in darkness and

in the shadow of death. Lord Jesus, come

soon!

—TAIZÉ PRAYER

Most gracious Son, may your teaching dispel the darkness of ignorance in our mind, and may your commands be beacons of light, showing us the path to peace. And as we walk on that oath, may we find your footprints on the ground, that we may place our own feet where you have trodden.

—Desiderius Erasmus

*L*ord, teach me to rest in you. Teach me to see the sky and to think of nothing else, but the joy of it. Teach me to look at field and flower and be soothed by colors and seasons. Teach me to close my eyes and to rest in the Love that has supported me all my days. Teach me, Lord, to rest in you.

—FRANK TOPPING

*S*tation 2: Jesus Receives and Carries His Cross.

We adore you, O Christ, and praise you, because by your holy Cross you have redeemed the world. O my Jesus, let me joyfully embrace your Cross and accept my own sufferings which pale beside yours.

—STATIONS OF THE CROSS

*L*ord, I want to

Go

where You want me to go

Do

what You want me to do

Be

what You want me to be

Save me!

—AFRICAN-AMERICAN SPIRITUAL

Blessed Lord, let me climb up near to Thee, and love, and long, and plead, and wrestle with Thee, and pant for deliverance from the body of sin, for my heart is wandering and lifeless, and my soul mourns to think it should ever lose sight of its beloved. Wrap my life in divine love, and keep me ever desiring Thee, always humble and resigned to Thy will, more fixed on Thyself, that I may be more fitted for doing and suffering.

—PURITAN PRAYER

The Cross is my sure salvation.

The Cross I ever adore.

The Cross of my Lord is with me.

The Cross is my refuge.

Amen.

—SAINT THOMAS AQUINAS

*M*ore things are wrought by

prayer than

this world dreams of.

—ALFRED, LORD TENNYSON

*L*ord, help me persist although I want to give up. Lord, help me to keep trying although I can't see what good it does. Lord, help me to keep praying although I'm not sure You hear me. Lord, help me to keep living in ways that seek to please You. Lord, help me to know when to lead and when to follow. Lord, help me to know when to speak and when to remain silent. Lord, help me to know when to act and when to wait.

—MARIAN WRIGHT EDELMAN

Almighty God, who art beyond the reach of our highest thought, and yet within the heart of the lowliest; come to us, we pray thee, in all the beauty of light, in all the tenderness of love, in all the liberty of truth. Mercifully help us to do justly, to love mercy, and to walk humbly with thee. Sanctify all our desires and purposes, and upon each of us let thy blessing rest, through Jesus Christ our Lord.

—PRAYER FROM SOUTH AFRICA

O Lord my God, I hope in thee;

My dear Lord Jesus, set me free;

In chains, in pains,

I long for thee.

On bended knee

I adore thee, implore thee

To set me free.

—MARY, QUEEN OF SCOTS

*G*racious and holy Father, give us wisdom to perceive you, intelligence to understand you, diligence to seek you, patience to wait on you, eyes to behold you, a heart to meditate on you, a life to proclaim you, through the power of the Spirit of Jesus Christ our Lord. Amen.

—BENEDICT OF NURSIA

*E*ternal God, the light of the minds
that know you, the joy of the hearts that
love you, the strength of the wills that
serve you; grant us so to know you that
we may truly love you, so to love you that
we may fully serve you, whom to serve is
perfect freedom, through Jesus Christ our
Lord. Amen.

—SAINT AUGUSTINE

*S*teer the ship of my life, good Lord, to your quiet harbour, where I can be safe from the storms of sin and conflict. Show me the course I should take. Renew in me the gift of discernment, so that I can always see the right direction in which I should go. And give me the strength and the courage to choose the right course, even when the sea is rough and the waves are high, knowing that through enduring hardship and danger in your name we shall find comfort and peace.

—BASIL THE GREAT

*D*ear Lord Jesus,

When I am too busy to pray, I deny that

  you are the center of my life.

When I neglect your Word,

I deny that you are competent

  to guide me.

When I worry, I deny that you are

  the Lord of circumstances.

When I turn my ear from the hungry and

  the homeless, I deny that you are a God of

  mercy who has put me here to be your

  hands and your feet.

Forgive me Jesus, for all those quiet ways,

known only to you, in which I have denied

you.

—KEN GIRE

*L*ord, You told me when I decided to follow You, You would walk and talk with me all the way. But I'm aware that during the most troublesome times of my life there is only one set of footprints. I just don't understand why, when I needed You most, You left me." He whispered, "My precious child, I love you and will never leave you, never, ever, during your trials and testings. When you saw only one set of footprints it was then that I carried you."

—MARGARET FISHBACK POWERS

*I*t is a good thing to let prayer be the first business of the morning and the last at night. Guard yourself carefully against those false, deluding ideas which tell you, "Wait a little while. I will pray in an hour; first I must attend to this or that." Such thoughts get you away from prayer into other affairs which so hold your attention and involve you that nothing comes of prayer that day.

—MARTIN LUTHER

Father, help me to be sensitive to what is happening to people around me. I know there are unmet needs beneath the surface of the most successful and self-assured. I know that today I will meet some who are enduring hidden physical or emotional pain, others who are fearful of an uncertain future, and still others who carry burdens of worry for families and friends. May I take no one for granted, but instead, be a ready communicator of Your love and encouragement. Make me aware of these concerns of others, available to express Your care, and articulate with Your hope.

—LLOYD JOHN OGILVIE

*D*ear God, be good to me;

the sea is so large,

and my boat is so small.

—PRAYER OF A

BRETON FISHERMAN

*C*ome and find the quiet center

In the crowded life we lead,

Find the room for hope to enter,

Find the frame where we are freed;

Clear the chaos and the clutter,

Clear our eyes, that we may see

All the things that really matter

Be at peace and simply be.

—SHIRLEY ERENA MURRAY

*A*s a deer thirsts for streams of

water, so I thirst for you, God.

I thirst for the living God. Where can I go

to meet with him?

—King David
Psalm 42:1–2 (NCV)

*M*ay the love of the Lord Jesus

　draw us to himself;

May the power of the Lord Jesus

　strengthen us in his service;

May the joy of the Lord Jesus

　fill our souls.

—WILLIAM TEMPLE

*O*f thy goodness, give us;

with thy love, inspire us;

by thy Spirit, guide us;

by thy power, protect us;

in thy mercy, receive us

now and always. Amen.

—FROM DIVINE WORSHIP

*W*ithout question, no other technique has been more valuable in aiding me to hear God's still small voice than journaling my dialogue with God.

—BOB JAPENGA

*P*raise to the Father,

Praise to the Son,

Praise to the Spirit,

The Three in One.

—CELTIC PRAYER

You keep us waiting.
You, the God of all time,
want us to wait
for the right time in which to discover
who we are, where we must go,
who will be with us, and what
    we must do.
So thank you . . . for the waiting time.

You keep us loving.
You, the God whose name is love,
want us to be like you—
to love the loveless and the unlovely
    and the unlovable;
to love without jealousy, or design or threat;
and, most difficult of all, to love ourselves.
So thank you . . . for the loving time.

—FROM THE IONA
COMMUNITY WORSHIP BOOK

*L*ord, temper with tranquility

Our manifold activity,

That we may do our work for thee

With very great simplicity.

—ASCRIBED TO A MEDIEVAL MONK

*D*ear God, here on earth you are constantly seeking to change us. At times we wish to flee into the wilderness to avoid you. But let us learn to love the lasting things of heaven, rather than the dying things of earth. We must accept that time always brings change; and we pray that by your grace the change within our souls will make us worthy of your heavenly kingdom, where all time will cease.

—ALCUIN OF YORK

And He walks with me,

And He talks with me,

And He tells me I am His own;

And the joy we share as we tarry there,

None other has ever known.

—CHARLES AUSTIN MILES

For food in a world

   where many walk in hunger;

For faith in a world

   where many walk in fear;

For friends in a world

   where many walk alone,

We give you humble thanks, O Lord.

—WORLD HUNGER GRACE

*D*ear Lord,

Before I go on up to bed,

And on my pillow lay my head,

I thank you, Lord, for the day I've had,

All the good times and the bad,

Thank you for the things I've seen,

And all the places I have been,

Thank you for my friends and relations

And all the people in different nations,

And as I come to this last verse,

I thank you for the universe.

—CHILDREN'S PRAYER

---

*L*ook upon us, O Lord, and let all
the darkness of our souls vanish before
the beams of your brightness. Fill us with
holy love, and open to us the treasures of
your wisdom. All our desire is known
unto you, therefore perfect what you have
begun, and what your Spirit has awak-
ened us to ask in prayer.

—SAINT AUGUSTINE

*T*here is nothing surer on this

earth than the truth that God

hears and answers prayer.

—LEANNE PAYNE

May our souls be lamps of yours,

kindled and illuminated by you.

May they shine and burn with the truth,

and never go out in darkness and ashes.

—MOZARABIC LITURGY

*A*lmighty God, who hast created us in thine own image, grant us grace fearlessly to contend against evil and to make no peace with oppression; and, that we may reverently use our freedom, help us to employ it in the maintenance of justice in our communities and among the nations, to the glory of thy holy Name; through Jesus Christ our Lord, who liveth and reigneth with thee and the Holy Spirit, One God, now and forever. Amen.

—COLLECT FOR SOCIAL SERVICE

Lord, you are my lover,

My longing,

My flowing stream,

My sun,

and I am your reflection.

—MECHTILD OF MAGDEBURG

*G*rant me, I beg you, almighty and most beautiful God, fervently to desire, wisely to search out, and perfectly to fulfill, all that is well-pleasing to you.

—SAINT THOMAS AQUINAS

Ah, dearest Jesus, Holy Child,

Make thee a bed, soft, undefiled,

Within my heart, that it may be

A quiet chamber kept for thee.

—MARTIN LUTHER

𝓛ord, make me according to thy heart.

—BROTHER LAWRENCE

*W*hen you pray do not try to express yourself in fancy words, for often it is the simple, repetitious phrases of a little child that our Father in heaven finds more irresistible. Do not strive for verbosity lest your mind be distracted from devotion by a search for words.

—SAINT JOHN CLIMACUS

O God, make the door of this house wide enough to receive all who need human love and fellowship, and a heavenly Father's care; and narrow enough to shut out all envy, pride and hate. Make its threshold smooth enough to be no stumbling-block to children, nor to straying feet, but rugged enough to turn back the tempter's power: make it a gateway to your eternal kingdom.

—THOMAS KEN

*G*od, I pray, light these idle sticks of my life and may I burn for you. Consume my life, my God, for it is yours. I seek not a long life, but a full one, like you, Lord Jesus.

—JIM ELLIOT

*M*y Lord Jesus Christ, two graces I beg of you before I die, the first is that in my lifetime I may feel, in my soul and in my body, as far as possible, that sorrow which you, sweet Jesus, endured in the hour of your most bitter passion, the second is that I may feel in my heart, as far as possible, that abundance of love with which you, Son of God, were inflamed, so as willingly to endure so great a passion for us sinners.

—SAINT FRANCIS OF ASSISI

*Y*ou called and cried out loud and shattered my deafness. You were radiant and resplendent, you put to flight my blindness. You were fragrant, and I drew in my breath and now pant after you. I tasted you, and I feel but hunger and thirst for you. You touched me, and I am set on fire to attain the peace which is yours.

—SAINT AUGUSTINE

O Brother Jesus, who wept at the death of a friend and overturned tables in anger at wrong let me not be frightened by the depths of passion. Rather let me learn the love and anger and wild expanses of soul within me that are true expressions of your grace and wisdom. And assure me again in becoming more like you I come closer to my true self made in the image of outpouring Love born of the free eternal Wind.

—CELTIC NIGHT PRAYER

I choose it all, my God. I do not want to become a saint by halves. I am not afraid of suffering for your sake. What I fear is holding on too tightly to my own will. So I give you everything; I want only what is your will for me.

—SAINT THERESE OF LISIEUX

*G*od of healing and wholeness, I invite your presence into the midst of my own incompleteness. Show clearly the reality of my brokenness and lead me now and always into your way of healing and wholeness. In the name of Jesus. Amen.

—REUBEN P. JOB

 $\mathcal{L}$ ord, I am not worthy

to receive you,

but only say the word

and I shall be healed.

—CATHOLIC TRADITIONAL

*T*he door of prayer has been

open ever since God made man in

his own image.

—GEORGE MACDONALD

*L*ord, help me today to realize that thou wilt be speaking to me through the events of the day, through people, through things, and through all creation. Give me ears, eyes and heart to perceive thee, however veiled thy presence may be. Give me insight to see through the exterior of things to the interior truth. Give me thy Spirit of discernment. O Lord, thou knowest how busy I must be this day. If I forget thee, do not thou forget me. Amen.

—SIR JACOB ASTLEY

*J*esus, my Shepherd,

Brother, Friend,

My Prophet, Priest, and King,

My Lord, my life, my way, my end,

Accept the praise I bring.

Weak is the effort of my heart,

And cold my warmest thought;

But when I see Thee as Thou art,

I'll praise Thee as I ought.

—JOHN NEWTON

From moral weakness of spirit;
from timidity; from hesitation, from fear
of others and dread of responsibility,
strengthen us with the courage to
speak the truth in love and self-control;
and alike from the weakness of hasty
violence and weakness of moral
cowardice, save us and help us,
we humbly beseech thee, O Lord.

—SOUTHWELL LITANY,

GEORGE RIDDING

O holy Child of Bethlehem,

Descend to us, we pray;

Cast out our sin and enter in,

Be born in us today.

We hear the Christmas angels

The great glad tidings tell;

O come to us, abide with us,

Our Lord Emmanuel!

—PHILLIPS BROOKS

O God of earth and altar,

Bow down and hear our cry,

Our earthly rulers falter,

Our people drift and die.

The walls of gold entomb us,

The sword of scorn divide,

Take not thy thunder from us,

But take away our pride.

—G. K. CHESTERTON

The Lord of the empty tomb, the conqueror of gloom, come to you. The Lord in the garden walking, the Lord to Mary talking, come to you. The Lord in the upper room, dispelling fear and doom, come to you. The Lord on the road to Emmaus, the Lord giving hope to Thomas, come to you. The Lord appearing on the shore, giving us life for evermore, come to you.

—DAVID ADAM

*L*ove of Jesus, fill us,

Joy of Jesus, surprise us,

Peace of Jesus, flood us,

Light of Jesus, transform us,

Touch of Jesus, warm us,

Strength of Jesus, encourage us,

O Saviour, in your agony, forgive us,

in your wounds, hide us,

and in your risen life take us with you, for

your love's sake.

—ANGELA ASHWIN

*L*ord Jesus, I know I am a sinner.
I believe you died for my sins. Right now,
I turn from my sins and open the door of
my heart and life. I receive you as my personal Lord and Savior. Thank you for
saving me now. Amen.

—BILLY GRAHAM

*C*hrist comes only in secret to those who have entered the inner chamber of the heart and closed the door behind them.

—THOMAS MERTON

*I*nfinite Lord, and eternal God,

rouse your church in this land,

restore your people's sense of mission,

and revive your work in holiness and

strength. By your Spirit, teach us to give

our energy, our time, our money, our

service and our prayer, that your

kingdom may be advanced; in the name

of Jesus Christ our Lord.

—CHURCH IN WALES

When my soul sheds its tears,

When my heart languishes in longing,

When my whole being shivers

   in fatigue,

Come, O Jesus, I beg you to come.

—A PRAYER WRITTEN BY
    LITHUANIAN PRISONERS

How easy, Lord, it is for me to live with you. How easy it is for me to believe in you. When my understanding is perplexed by doubts or on the point of giving up, when the most intelligent men see no further than the coming evening, and know not what they shall do tomorrow, you send me a clear assurance that you are there and that you will ensure that not all the roads of goodness are barred.

From the heights of earthly fame I look
back in wonder at the road that led
through hopelessness to this place whence
I can send mankind a reflection of your
radiance. And whatever I in this life may
yet reflect, that you will give me; and
whatever I shall not attain, that, plainly,
you have purposed for others.

—ALEKSANDR SOLZHENITSYN

O Jesus,

Be the canoe that holds me

in the sea of life.

Be the steer that keeps me straight.

Be the outrigger that supports me

in times of great temptation.

Let your Spirit be my sail that

carries me through each day.

Keep my body strong,

so that I can paddle steadfastly on,

in the long voyage of life.

—A NEW HEBRIDEAN PRAYER

*L*et there be

respect for the earth,

peace for its people,

love in our lives,

delight in the good,

forgiveness for past wrongs,

and from now on a new start.

—THE MILLENNIUM RESOLUTION

*L*ord, help me to enjoy the common things of my everyday life. I often find myself saying that nothing happened today, when in fact the ordinary events of my life make a rich pattern, but they are so familiar I hardly notice them, things like cups of tea and coffee and meals shared with friends and colleagues; or listening to favorite family stories that we have heard and told so often. Lord of Life, help me to recognize the joy of simple things.

—FRANK TOPPING

Dear Lord, give me truths which are veiled by the doctrines and articles of faith, which are masked by pious words of sermons and books. Let my eyes penetrate the veil, and tear off the mask, that I can see your truth face to face.

—Saint John of the Cross

*T*here is no other perfect
meditation than the saving
and blessed Name of Our Lord
Jesus Christ dwelling without
interruption in you.

—SAINT MACARIUS

*C*ome now, little man, turn aside

for a while from your daily employment,

escape for a moment

from the tumult of your thoughts.

Put aside your weighty cares,

let your burdensome distractions wait,

free yourself awhile for God,

and rest awhile in Him.

Enter the inner chamber of your soul,

shut out everything except God

and that which can help you in seeking Him,

and when you have shut the door, seek Him.

Now, my whole heart, say to God,

"I seek your face,

Lord, it is your face I seek."

—SAINT ANSELM

*S*et a guard, O Lord, at the door of my lips, that I may speak nothing inconsistent with perfect truth and love.

—F. B. MEYER

*B*ring us, O Lord God, at the last
awakening into the house and gate of
heaven, to enter into that gate and dwell
in that house, where there shall be no
darkness nor dazzling, but one equal light;
no noise nor silence, but one equal music;
no fears nor hopes, but an equal posses-
sion; no ends nor beginnings, but one
equal eternity, in the habitations of thy
majesty and thy glory, world without end.

—JOHN DONNE

*S*tation 3: Jesus Falls under the Weight of the Cross for the First Time.

We adore you, O Christ, and praise you, because by your holy Cross you have redeemed the world. Dear Lord, by this your first fall, raise us all out of sin who have so miserably fallen under its power. Help me to take up my own cross and follow you.

—STATIONS OF THE CROSS

*W*hen sweeping floors: I pray thee, Lord, to sweep away my heart's uncleanness, that my heart may always be pure. When watering flowers: I pray thee, Lord, to send down spiritual rain into my heart, to germinate the good seed there. When boiling water for tea: I pray thee, Lord, to send down spiritual fire to burn away the coldness of my heart and that I may always be hot-hearted in serving thee.

—CHINESE PRAYER

*G*rant Lord, that I may not, for one moment, admit willingly into my soul any thought contrary to thy love.

—E. B. PUSEY

*P*rayer is not conquering
God's reluctance, but taking hold
of God's willingness.

—PHILLIPS BROOKS

May the flames of thy love

ever blaze upon the altar of my heart.

—CHARLES DEVANESAN

*M*ay the Lord bless you with all
good and keep you from all evil; may He
give light to your heart with loving wisdom, and be gracious to you with eternal
knowledge; may He lift up His loving
countenance upon you for
eternal peace.

—DEAD SEA SCROLLS

May the road rise up to meet you.

May the wind be always at your back.

May the sun shine warm upon your face;

the rains fall softly upon your fields; and

until we meet again, may God hold you

in the palm of his hand.

—OLD GAELIC BLESSING

*C*ome, true light.

Come, life eternal.

Come, hidden mystery.

Come, treasure without name.

Come, reality beyond all words.

Come, person beyond understanding.

Come, rejoicing without end.

Come, light that knows no evening.

Come, unfailing expectation of the
    saved.

Come, raising of the fallen.

Come, resurrection of the dead. . . .

Come, for you are yourself the desire
    that is within me.

—SAINT SYMEON THE NEW
                THEOLOGIAN

$\mathcal{N}$ow unto the King eternal, immortal, invisible, the only wise God, be honor and glory forever and ever.

—1 TIMOTHY 1:17 (KJV)

Today he who hung the earth upon the waters is hung upon the Cross. He who is King of the angels is arrayed in a crown of thorns. He who wraps the heaven in clouds is wrapped in the purple of mockery. He who in Jordan set Adam free receives blows upon his face. The Bridegroom of the Church is transfixed with nails. The Son of the Virgin is pierced with a spear. We venerate the Passion, O Christ. Show us also thy glorious Resurrection.

—HYMNS FOR GOOD FRIDAY,
ORTHODOX

The things, good Lord, that we pray for, give us the grace to labor for.

—SAINT THOMAS MORE

Today, O Lord,

I yield myself to you.

May your will be my delight today.

May your way have perfect sway in me.

May your love be the pattern

of my living.

—RICHARD FOSTER

*H*e prays constantly who unites prayer with the deeds required and mixes deeds with prayer. For the only way we can accept the command of St. Paul to pray constantly as referring to a real possibility is by saying that the entire life of the saint taken as a whole is a single great prayer.

—ORIGEN OF ALEXANDRIA

O God,

who hast so greatly loved us,

and mercifully redeemed us;

give us grace that in everything

we may yield ourselves,

our wills and our works,

a continual thank offering unto thee,

through Jesus Christ our Lord. Amen.

—WESTMINSTER DIVINES

*T*o God the Father, who first loved us

and made us accepted in the Beloved:

To God the Son, who loved us, and

washed us from our sins in his own blood;

To God the Holy Ghost, who sheds the

love of God abroad in our hearts,

Be all love and all glory,

From time and all eternity.

—THOMAS KEN

I pray for these followers, but I am also praying for all those who will believe in me because of their teaching. Father, I pray that they can be one. As you are in me and I am in you, I pray that they can also be one in us. Then the world will believe that you sent me. I have given these people the glory that you gave me so that they can be one, just as you and I are one. I will be in them and you will be in me so that they will be completely one. Then the world will know that you sent me and that you loved them just as much as you loved me.

—JESUS
GOSPEL OF JOHN 17:20–23 (NCV)

*H*oly Spirit of God, who prefers
before all temples the upright heart and
pure, instruct us in all truth; what is dark,
illumine, what is low, raise and support,
what is shallow, deepen; that every chap-
ter in our lives may witness to your power
and justify the ways of God.

—JOHN MILTON

O our God, grant us the grace to seek
first the kingdom of God. Let this quest
be our first thought on waking, our last
before sleeping. Let it govern all our deci-
sions, and all our plans

concerning the education of our children,
the choice of their vocation,

getting them established. Let it decide the
orientation of our life, let it occupy the
central place.

—MADAME MIRABAUD

Lord Jesus,

Bless all who serve us,

who have dedicated their lives

to the ministry of others—

all the teachers of our schools

who labor so patiently with

so little appreciation;

all who wait upon the public,

the clerks in the stores who have to accept

criticism, complaints, bad

manners, and selfishness

at the hands of a thoughtless public.

Bless the mailman, the drivers of

streetcars and buses who must listen to

people who lose their tempers.

Bless every humble soul who, in these

days of stress and strain,

preaches sermons

without words. Amen.

—PETER MARSHALL

*G*od of our life, through all the circling years, we trust in Thee; in all the past, through all our hopes and fears, Thy hand we see. With each new day, when morning lifts the veil, we own Thy mercies, Lord, which never fail.

—HUGH THOMSON KERR

A man is powerful

on his knees.

—CORRIE TEN BOOM

*A*t Tara today in this fateful hour
I place all heaven within its power
And the sun with its brightness
And the snow with its whiteness
And the fire with all the strength it hath,
And lightning with its rapid wrath,
And the winds with their swiftness
    along their path,
And the sea with its deepness,
And the earth with its starkness.
All these I place,
By God's almighty grace,
Between myself and the powers of
    darkness.

—SAINT PATRICK

*W*e are tired, Lord,
weary of the long night without rest.
We grow complaining and bitter.
We sorrow for ourselves as we grow hard-
ened to the pain of others. Another death
leaves us unmoved.
A widow's tears fall unnoticed. Our
children know only the bitterness already
possessing their parents. Our violent
words explode into violent acts by the
hands of our youth bringing destruction
without thought or reason. Lord, have
mercy upon us. Lead us to repentance
that we may forgive and be forgiven.
Amen.

—THOMAS A. PATTERSON

*W*ho but you, Lord, could bring sweetness in the midst of bitterness, pleasure in the midst of torment? How wonderful are the wounds in my soul, since the deeper the wound, the greater is the joy of healing.

—SAINT JOHN OF THE CROSS

O God:

Enlarge my heart that it may be big enough to receive the greatness of your love.

Stretch my heart that it may take into it all those who with me around the world believe in Jesus Christ. Stretch it that it may take into it all those who do not know him, but who are my responsibility because I know him. And stretch it that it may take into it all those who are not lovely in my eyes, and whose hands I do not want to touch, through Jesus Christ, my Savior. Amen.

—KAPINGA ESETE

---

*T*oday, O God,

the soles of your feet have touched the earth.

Today, the back street, the

forgotten place have been lit up with

significance. Today, the households of earth

welcome the King of heaven.

For you have come among us; you are one of

us. So may our songs rise to surround your

throne as our knees bend to salute your

cradle. Amen.

—CHURCH OF SCOTLAND

*I*f we are too impatient to finish the

work we have begun,

If we are too impatient to listen to someone

who wants to

Talk to us, or to give someone a helping

hand;

If we think that other people are fools, and

make no attempt to conceal our

contempt for them,

Forgive us, O God.

—WILLIAM BARCLAY

*W*e beseech thee, O Lord, mercifully to correct our wanderings; and by the guiding radiance of thy compassion to bring us to the saving vision of thy truth.

—GOTHIC MISSAL

*S*un and moon, bless the Lord;
fire and heat, bless the Lord;
winter and summer, bless the Lord;
praise him and magnify him forever.

Dew and frosts, bless the Lord;
frosts and cold, bless the Lord;
ice and snow, bless the Lord;
praise him and magnify him forever.

Nights and days, bless the Lord;
light and darkness, bless the Lord;
lightning and clouds, bless the Lord;
praise him and magnify him forever.

Let the earth bless the Lord;
mountains and hills, bless the Lord;
all green things on earth, bless the Lord;
praise him and magnify him forever.

—MEDIEVAL PRYMER

*E*very great movement of God

can be traced to a kneeling figure.

—D. L. MOODY

*J*esus, Son of the living God, splendor
of the Father, eternal light.

Lord, we praise you!

Jesus, Wonderful Counselor, Everlasting Lord,
Prince of Peace.

Lord, we praise you!

Jesus, God of peace, friend of all, source of
life and of holiness.

Lord, we praise you!

Jesus, brother of the poor, goodness without
measure, inexhaustible wisdom.

Lord, we praise you!

Jesus, good shepherd, true light, our way
and our life.

Lord, we praise you!

—TAIZE PRAYER

I weave a silence on my lips,

I weave a silence into my mind,

I weave a silence within my heart,

I close my ears to distractions,

I close my eyes to attentions,

I close my heart to temptations.

Calm me, O Lord, as you stilled the storm,

Still me, O Lord, keep me from harm.

Let all tumult within me cease,

Enfold me, Lord, in your peace.

—CELTIC TRADITIONAL

I asked for strength that I might achieve; I was made weak that I might learn humbly to obey. I asked for health that I might do greater things; I was given infirmity that I might do better things. I asked for riches that I might be happy; I was given poverty that I might be wise. I asked for power that I might have the praise of men; I was given weakness that I might feel the need of God. I asked for all things that I might enjoy life; I was given life that I might enjoy all things. I got nothing that I had asked for, but everything that I had hoped for. Almost despite myself my
unspoken prayers were answered; I am, among all men, most richly blessed.

—UNKNOWN CONFEDERATE SOLDIER

O Lord, I am yours. Do what seems good in your sight, and give me complete resignation to your will.

—DAVID LIVINGSTONE

Father, give me the courage to overcome all those fears that would rise within me saying, "I am not sure that I can face it." Deepen the conviction within me that with You, I can face anything.

—SELWYN HUGHES

*L*ord, I do not know what to ask of you; only you know what I need. I simply present myself to you; I open my heart to you. I have no other desire than to accomplish your will. Teach me to pray. Amen.

—FRANÇOIS DE FÉNELON

We Taste Thee, O Thou Living
   Bread,

And long to feast upon Thee still;

We drink of Thee, the fountainhead

And thirst our souls from Thee to fill.

—SAINT BERNARD

*S*o shall it be at last,

in that bright morning

When the soul waketh,

and life's shadows flee;

Oh, in that hour,

fairer than day-light dawning,

Shall rise the glorious thought—

I am with Thee.

—HARRIET BEECHER STOWE

A teardrop on earth summons

the King of Heaven.

—CHARLES SWINDOLL

*G*rant me, O Lord, heavenly wisdom, that I might learn to seek you above all things, and to understand all other things as they are according to the order of your wisdom. Amen.

—THOMAS À KEMPIS

May the strength of God pilot me.

May the power of God preserve me. May

the wisdom of God instruct me. May the

hand of God protect me.

May the way of God direct me.

May the shield of God defend me.

—SAINT PATRICK

O Lord, baptize our hearts into a

sense of the conditions and needs of all

men.

—GEORGE FOX

*O*pen my eyes, that I may see

Glimpses of truth Thou hast for me;

Place in my hands the wonderful key

That shall unclasp and set me free.

—CLARA H. SCOTT

Merciful God,

In your love for us, your children,

You inspired St. Nicholas

To deeds of kindness and compassion
   for the poor.

Help us, after his example,

To serve the poor, the hungry,

The dispossessed, and the lonely

In the true spirit of the Gospel.

Give us the grace

To walk in the footsteps of the Gospel

Without fear,

And to proclaim it with joy

All the days of our lives.

—BYZANTINE VESPERS ON
SAINT NICHOLAS

*H*elp the offbeat,

Capture their rebellion,

Listen to their song of forsakenness,

Reach them in their exile.

But let some of their courage rub off

   on me, Lord.

I don't want to be swallowed up by the

   whale of conformity.

—JEANETTE STRUCHEN

*F*ig trees may not grow figs, and there may be no grapes on the vines. There may be no olives growing and no food growing in the fields. There may be no sheep in the pens and no cattle in the barns. But I will still be glad in the Lord; I will rejoice in God my Savior. The Lord is my strength. He makes me like a deer that does not stumble so I can walk on the steep mountains.

—HABAKKUK THE PROPHET,
HABAKKUK 3:17–19 (NCV)

*A*lmighty and most merciful God, we remember before you all poor and neglected persons whom it would be easy for us to forget: the homeless and destitute, the old and the sick, and all who have none to care for them. Help us to heal those who are broken in body or spirit, and to turn their sorrow into joy. Grant this, Father, for the love of your Son, who for our sake became poor, Jesus Christ our Lord. Amen.

—BOOK OF COMMON PRAYER

*I*f you are seeking after God,

you may be sure of this: God is

seeking you much more.

—SAINT JOHN OF THE CROSS

*G*od, you are my God. I search for you. I thirst for you like someone in a dry, empty land where there is no water. I have seen you in the Temple and have seen your strength and glory. Because your love is better than life, I will praise you. I will praise you as long as I live. I will lift up my hands in prayer to your name. I will be content as if I had eaten the best foods. My lips will sing, and my mouth will praise you. I remember you while I'm lying in bed; I think about you through the night. You are my help. Because of your protection, I sing. I stay close to you; you support me with your right hand.

—KING DAVID
PSALM 63:1–8 (NCV)

Jesus, I am resting, resting

In the joy of what Thou art;

I am finding out the greatness

Of Thy loving heart.

Thou hast bid me gaze upon Thee,

And Thy beauty fills my soul,

For by Thy transforming power,

Thou hast made me whole.

—JEAN SOPHIA PIGOTT

ℒord of new beginnings, help me to

be among those who encourage others to

a spiritual awakening. Count me among

those of Your children who pray for the

needs of those whose understanding is

darkened.

—LLOYD JOHN OGILVIE

*G*ive us strength, O Lord we pray
   to travel on from day to day.
Along the path that leads until
   we reach full union with your will.

We've traveled far, but oh! we know
   we have a long, long way to go.
While there is pain, adversity
   throughout the world
   we plainly see
Our work for you is far from done.
   Indeed, it hardly has begun.

—HANNAH HURNARD

*A*bide with me—fast falls
   the eventide;
the darkness deepens—Lord, with
   me abide;
When other helpers fail, and comforts flee,
Help of the helpless, O abide with me.

Hold Thou Thy cross before my
   closing eyes,
Shine thru the gloom and point me to
   the skies;
Heaven's morning breaks and earth's
   vain shadows flee:
In life, in death, O Lord, abide with me.

—HENRY FRANCIS LYTE

Alone with none but thee, my God,

I journey on my way.

What need I fear, when thou art near,

O king of night and day?

More safe am I within thy hand

Than if a host did round me stand.

—SAINT COLUMBA

*T*o every cry from your passion-

filled hearts, God replies, "Christ."

—LARRY CRABB

*L*et nothing trouble you.

Let nothing scare you.

All is fleeting.

God alone is unchanging.

Patience

Everything obtains.

Who possesses God

Nothing wants.

God alone suffices.

—SAINT TERESA OF AVILA

'Tis true, we are but strangers

and sojourners below;

And countless snares and dangers

surround the path we go.

Though painful and distressing,

yet there's a rest above,

And onward we are pressing

to reach that land of love.

—THE BELIEVER'S
DAILY TREASURE

Dear Jesus, though there was no room for you in the inn, grant this day that I might make abundant room for you in my heart.

—KEN GIRE

*G*od the Father, bless us;

God the Son, defend us;

God the Spirit, keep us

Now and evermore.

—FROM LITTLE FOLDED HANDS

Our God, God of all men,

God of heaven and earth, seas

   and rivers,

God of sun and moon, of all the stars,

God of high mountains and lowly valleys,

God over heaven, and in heaven,

   and under heaven.

He has a dwelling in heaven and earth

   and sea

   and in all things that are in them.

He inspires all things, he quickens

   all things

He is over all things, he supports

   all things.

He makes the light of the sun to shine,

He surrounds the moon and the stars,

He has made wells in the arid earth,

Placed dry islands in the sea.

He has a Son co-eternal with himself,

And the Holy Spirit breathes in them;

Not separate are the Father and the Son

and the Holy Spirit.

—SAINT PATRICK

*L*ord Jesus,

I give thee my hands to do thy work.

I give thee my feet to go thy way.

I give thee my eyes to see as thou seest.

I give thee my tongue to speak they words.

I give thee my mind that thou mayest
    think in me.

I give thee my spirit that thou mayest
    pray in me.

Above all, I give thee my heart that thou
    mayest love in me
      thy Father and all mankind.

I give thee my whole self that thou mayest
    grow in me, so that it is thee,

Lord Jesus, who lives and works and prays
    in me.

—LANCELOT ANDREWS

The way, not mine, O Lord,
However dark it be;
Lead me by thine own hand,
Choose out the path for me.
Smooth let it be or rough,
It will be still the best;
Winding or straight, it leads
Right onward to thy rest.
Choose thou for me my friends,
My sickness or my health;
Choose thou my cares for me,
My poverty or wealth.
Not mine, not mine the choice
In things great or small;
Be thou my guide, my strength,
My wisdom and my all.

—HORATIUS BONAR

*L*ord, as I read the Psalms, let me hear you singing. As I read your words, let me hear you speaking. As I reflect on each page, let me see your image. And as I seek to put your precepts into practice, let my heart be filled with joy.

—SAINT GREGORY

OF NAZIANZUS

I am bending my knee

In the eye of the Father who created me,

In the eye of the Son who purchased me,

In the eye of the Spirit who cleansed me,

in friendship and affection.

—CARMINA GADELICA

O Almighty God, the Father of all humanity, turn, we pray, the hearts of all peoples and their rulers, that by the power of your Holy Spirit peace may be established among the nations on the foundation of justice, righteousness and truth; through him who was lifted up on the cross to draw all people to himself, your Son Jesus Christ our Lord. Amen.

—WILLIAM TEMPLE

*G*rant me to recognize in other men,

Lord God, the radiance of your own face.

—PIERRE TEILHARD DE CHARDIN

God,

Anything You have ever done,

You can do now.

Anything You have done anywhere else,

You can do here.

Anything You have done for anyone else,

You can do for me.

—THE HOPE PRAYER

*Y*ou were despised and rejected of
men, O Lord; a man of sorrows and
acquainted with grief, so you can understand when I feel rejected; you can feel my
sorrow and sadness.

I thank you for your presence
    in all my times of darkness,
        and for giving me light along the way.

—DENIS DUNCAN

I love you, O God,

my Love,

my Warmth,

my Solace,

my Fulfillment,

All that I am,

all that I do

finds meaning and purpose in you.

Fill me with the full force

of your Love

and its passionate splendor,

so that I might hold

and heal all those who are crying out for

 love.

Love through me

all the unreconciled

whose homes and hearts

are broken,

and let them know

I am able to love

because you have first loved me.

—MIRIAM THERESE WINTER

*A*ccept my prayers, dear Father, for those who have no one to love them enough to pray for them. Wherever and whoever they are, give them a share of my blessings, and in thy love let them know that they are not forgotten.

—SAINT FRANCIS OF ASSISI

*A*sk, and it will be given to you; seek, and you will find; knock, and it will be opened to you. For everyone who asks receives, and he who seeks finds, and to him who knocks it will be opened. Or what man is there among you who, if his son asks for bread, will give him a stone? Or if he asks for a fish, will give him a serpent? If you then, being evil, know how to give good gifts to your children, how much more will your Father who is in heaven give good things to those who ask Him!

—JESUS
MATTHEW 7:7–11 (NKJV)

*Y*ou have made us for yourself and
our hearts are restless until they find their
rest in you.

—Saint Augustine

Holy and eternal God,

give us such trust in your sure

purpose,

that we measure our lives

not by what we have done or

failed to do,

but by our faithfulness to you.

—ANGLICAN CHURCH
A NEW ZEALAND PRAYER BOOK

$\mathcal{G}$od, stay with me; let no word cross my

lips that is not your word, no thoughts enter

my mind that are not your thoughts, no

deed ever be done or entertained by me

that is not your deed.

—MALCOLM MUGGERIDGE

O Lord, that lends me life,

Lend me a heart replete with

thankfulness.

—WILLIAM SHAKESPEARE

*A*s the rain hides the stars, as the autumn mist hides the hills, as the clouds veil the blue of the sky, so the dark happenings of my lot hide the shining of your face from me. Yet, if I may hold your hand in the darkness, it is enough. Since I know that, though I may stumble in my going, you do not fall.

—CELTIC ORAL TRADITION

May my mouth praise the love of

God this morning.

O God, may I do your will this day.

May my ears hear the words of God and

obey them.

O God, may I do your will this day.

May my feet follow the footsteps of God

this day.

O God, may I do your will this day.

—PRAYER FROM JAPAN

*T*he prayer life does not consist
of perpetual repetition of petitions.
The prayer life consists of life that
is always upward and onward and
Godward.

—G. CAMPBELL MORGAN

Almighty and everlasting God, who enkindles the flame of your love in the hearts of the saints, grant to our minds the same faith and power and love; that as we rejoice in their triumphs, we may profit by their examples; through Jesus Christ our Lord. Amen.

—GOTHIC MISSAL

*L*ord, high and holy, meek and lowly,
Thou hast brought me to the valley of vision,
where I live in the depths but see Thee in the
heights; hemmed in by mountains of sin I
behold Thy glory. Let me learn by paradox that
the way down is the way up, that to be low is to
be high, that the broken heart is the healed
heart, that the contrite spirit is the rejoicing spirit, that the repenting soul is the victorious soul,
that to have nothing is to possess all, that to
bear the cross is to wear the crown, that to give
is to receive, that the valley is the place of
vision.

—THE VALLEY OF VISION,
PURITAN PRAYER

I arise today

Through a mighty strength:

> God's power to guide me,
>
> God's might to uphold me,
>
> God's wisdom to teach me,
>
> God's eyes to watch over me,
>
> God's ear to hear me,
>
> God's word to give me speech,
>
> God's hand to guard me,
>
> God's way to lie before me,
>
> God's shield to shelter me,
>
> God's host to shield me.

—SAINT BRIDGID OF IRELAND

*P*raise be to You, my Lord, for all
your Creatures, above all, Brother Sun
who gives us the light of day. For he is
beautiful, and radiant with great splendor, and so is like You, most high Lord.

Praise be to You, my Lord, for Sister
Moon and the stars. In heaven You
fashioned them, clear and precious
and beautiful.

Praise be to You, my Lord, for Brother
Wind, and for every kind of weather,
cloudy or fair, stormy or serene, by
which You cherish all that you have
made.

Praise be to You, my Lord, for Sister
   Water, which is useful and humble
   and precious and pure.
Praise be to You, my Lord, for Brother
   Fire, by whom You lighten the night,
   for he is beautiful and playful and
   robust and strong.
Praise be to You, my Lord, for our Sister
   Earth, who sustains and governs us,
   and produces varied fruits with
   colored flowers and herbs.

—SAINT FRANCIS OF ASSISI

*L*et me bless almighty God, whose power extends over sea and land, whose angels watch over all. Let me study sacred books to calm my soul; I pray for peace, kneeling at heaven's gates. Let me do my daily work, gathering seaweed, catching fish, giving food to the poor. Let me say my daily prayers, sometimes chanting, sometimes quiet, always thanking God. Delightful it is to live on a peaceful isle, in a quiet cell, serving the King of kings.

—Saint Columba's Rock

Lord, take my heart,

for I cannot give it to you.

And when you have it,

keep it.

For I would not take it from you.

—FRANÇOIS DE FÉNELON

*D*eep peace of the shining star

 to you,

Deep peace of the running wave

 to you,

Deep peace of the quiet earth to you,

Deep joy of the leaping fire to you,

Deep peace of the Son of Peace

 to you.

—WELSH BLESSING

*T*here is a place where thou canst touch the eyes of blinded men to instant, perfect sight; there is a place where thou canst say, "Arise" to dying captives, bound in chains of night; there is a place where thou canst reach the store of hoarded gold and free it for the Lord; there is a place—upon some distant shore— where thou canst send the worker and the Word. Where is that secret place—dost thou ask, "Where?" O soul, it is the secret place of prayer!

—ALFRED, LORD TENNYSON

God bless you and keep you.

May God smile on you, and be

merciful to you;

May God turn his regard toward you

and give you peace.

—SAINT FRANCIS OF ASSISI

*L*ord, because I am the lowliest of creatures, You have raised me to Yourself.

Lord, because I have no earthly treasures,
You have poured upon me heavenly
wealth.

Lord, because I am dressed in the grey rags
of flaws,

You have clothed me in the pure white robe
of grace.

Lord, because I desire the merest hut for
my home,
You have welcomed me to Your eternal
palace.

—MECHTHILD OF MAGDEBURG

*B*less this house, O Lord, we pray.

Let your joy shine here today.

Fill each corner with Your grace.

Make this home a peaceful place.

Let laughter ring throughout the hall.

Bring harmony to these four walls.

May all who enter be at rest

   as Your love touches each and

   every guest.

—NANCY LYNCH WEISS,

"A HOUSE BLESSING"

*I*n this time of sorrow

Help us to remember and know

Deeply,

That if we simply turn to You

Our hearts will be comforted

Our loads will be lightened

Our souls will be understood.

—JENNIFER M. SPENCER

*A*ll through this day, O Lord,

by the power of thy quickening Spirit,

let me touch the lives of others for good,

whether through the word I speak, the

prayer I speak or the life I live.

—ANCIENT COLLECT

*H*eavenly Sower, plow me first, and then sow the truth in me. Let me produce a bountiful harvest for You. Amen.

—CHARLES SPURGEON

*C*hrist leads me through no darker

  rooms

Than he went through before;

He that into God's kingdom comes

Must enter by this door.

—RICHARD BAXTER

*T*each me to feel another's Woe,

To hide the Fault I see;

That Mercy I to others show,

That Mercy show to me.

—ALEXANDER POPE

*E*very morning lean thine

arms awhile

Upon the window sill of heaven

And gaze upon thy Lord,

Then, with vision in thy heart,

Turn strong to meet thy day.

—THOMAS BLAKE

I pray God may open your eyes and let you see what hidden treasures he bestows on us in the trials from which the world thinks only to flee.

—JOHN OF AVILA

*S*tation 12: Jesus Dies Upon the Cross.

We adore you, O Christ, and praise you, because by your holy Cross you have redeemed the world. O my God and Father, you have valued us so much you were willing to pay the highest of all possible prices for our sinful souls. Should we not love and choose you above all things as the one necessary and only good?

—STATIONS OF THE CROSS

*D*ear God, let my hands be always hands of healing through which Your life may radiate to lessen pain, to bring a renewal of peace and healing wherever needed.

Dear God, let my hands bring through their touch some essence of Your love flowing through them to bring comfort and joy. I offer my hands as a channel; use them as Your healing tools.

—ELIZABETH SEARLE LAMB

*T*he stillness of God be mine this night

—that I may sleep in peace.

The awareness of the angels be mine

this night—

that I may be alert to unseen mysteries.

The company of the saints be mine this

night—

that I may dream of the river of love.

The life of Christ be mine this night—

that I may be truly alive to the morning

That I may be truly alive.

—CELTIC NIGHT PRAYER

*Y*ou are standing before God in the presence of the host of angels. The Holy Spirit is about to set his seal on each of your souls. You are about to be drawn into the service of the great king.

—CYRIL OF JERUSALEM

I am only a spark
Make me a fire.
I am only a string
Make me a lyre.
I am only a drop
Make me a fountain.
I am only a hill
Make me a mountain.
I am only a feather
Make me a wing.
I am only a rag
Make me a king!

—PRAYER FROM MEXICO

*B*e anxious for nothing,

but in everything by prayer and

supplication, with thanksgiving,

let your requests be made known

to God; and the peace of God,

which surpasses all understanding,

will guard your hearts and minds

through Christ Jesus.

—SAINT PAUL

PHILIPPIANS 4:6–7 (NKJV)

O God, make the door of this house wide enough to receive all who need human love and fellowship; narrow enough to shut out all envy, pride and strife. Make its threshold smooth enough to be no stumbling block to children, nor to straying feet, but rugged and strong enough to turn back the tempter's power. God make the door of this house the gateway to thine eternal kingdom.

—ON SAINT STEPHEN'S
WALBROOK, LONDON

Holy, holy, holy,

Lord God Almighty,

Who was and is and is to come! . . .

You are worthy, O Lord,

To receive glory and honor and power;

For You created all things,

And by Your will they exist and were

   created.

—SAINT JOHN
REVELATION 4:8, 11 (NKJV)

*H*eavenly Father,

Help us remember that the jerk who cut us off in traffic last night is a single mother who worked nine hours that day and is rushing home to cook dinner, help with homework, do the laundry and spend a few precious moments with her children.

Help us to remember that the pierced, tattooed, disinterested young man who can't make change correctly is a worried 19-year-old college student, balancing his apprehension over final exams with his fear of not getting his student loans for next semester.

Remind us, Lord, that the scary-looking bum, begging for money in the same spot every day (who really ought to get a job!) is a slave to addictions that we can only imagine in our worst nightmares.

Help us to remember that the old couple walking annoyingly slow through the store aisles and blocking our shopping progress are savoring this moment, knowing that, based on the biopsy report she got back last week, this will be the last year that they go shopping together.

Heavenly Father, remind us each day that, of all the gifts you give us, the greatest gift is love. It is not enough to share that love with those we hold dear. Open our hearts not to just those who are close to us, but to all humanity. Let us be slow to judge and quick to forgive, show patience, empathy and love.

—ANONYMOUS

O God, be all my love, all my hope, all my striving; let my thoughts and words flow from you, my daily life be in you, and every breath I take be in you. Amen.

—JOHN CASSIAN

*A*wake, my soul, and with the sun
Thy daily stage of duty run;
Shake off dull sloth, and joyful rise
To pay Thy morning sacrifice.

Lord, I my vows to Thee renew;
Disperse my sins as morning dew;
Guard my first springs of thought and will,
And with Thyself my spirit fill.

Direct, control, suggest, this day,
All I design to do or say;
That all my pow'rs, with all their might,
In Thy sole glory may unite.

Praise God, from whom all blessings flow;
Praise Him, all creatures here below;
Praise Him above, ye heavenly host;
Praise Father, Son, and Holy Ghost.

—THOMAS KEN

*M*y God, the spring of all

   my joys,

The life of my delights,

The glory of my brightest days,

And comfort of my nights!

In darkest shades, if thou appear,

My dawning is begun;

Thou art my soul's bright morning star,

And thou my rising sun.

—Isaac Watts

*S*oul of Christ, sanctify me.

Body of Christ, heal me.

Blood of Christ, drench me.

Water from the side of Christ, wash me.

Passion of Christ, strengthen me.

Good Jesus, hear me.

In your wounds shelter me.

From turning away keep me.

From the evil one protect me.

At the hour of my death call me.

Into your presence lead me,

to praise you with all your saints

forever and ever.

Amen.

—ANIMA CHRISTI

*T*he whole meaning of prayer is that we may know God.

—OSWALD CHAMBERS

*A*s watchmen wait for the
morning, so do our souls long for you,
O Christ. Come with the dawning of the
day, and make yourself known to us in
the breaking of bread; for you are our
God for ever and ever. Amen.

—MOZARABIC MORNING PRAYER

*G*rant us, O God, your protection;
and in your protection, strength; and in
strength, understanding; and in understanding, knowledge; and in knowledge,
the knowledge of justice; and in the
knowledge of justice, the love of justice;
and in that love, the love of existence; and
in the love of existence, the love of God,
God and all goodness.

—WELSH PRAYER

*G*od the Father bless me, Christ guard me, the Holy Spirit enlighten me, all the days of my life. The Lord be my defender and guardian of my soul and my body, now and ever, and world without end. Amen.

—FROM THE BOOK OF CERNE

*L*ord, let Thy glory be my end, Thy word my rule, and then Thy will be done.

—KING CHARLES II

Prayer is the mother and
daughter of tears. It is an expiation
of sin, a bridge across temptation,
a bulwark against affliction. It
wipes out conflict, is the work of
angels, and is the nourishment
of everything spiritual.

—SAINT JOHN CLIMACUS

Thank you, Lord, that even though we fail you, you never give up on us.

—RON BRANDON

Almighty God, you are Lord of time
and have neither beginning nor end: you
are the redeemer of souls, the foundation
of human reason and guardian of our
hearts; through all that you have created
you have revealed your indescribable
power; receive, O Lord, our supplication
even at this hour of the night, provide fully
for the needs of each of us and make us
worthy of your goodness. For your name is
worthy of all honor and greatness and is to
be glorified with hymns of blessing, Father,
Son and Holy Spirit, now and for ever, to
the ages of ages. Amen.

—GREEK ORTHODOX MONASTIC

*B*ehold, O kind and most sweet Jesus, I cast myself upon my knees in your sight, and with the most fervent desire of my soul I pray and beseech you that you would impress upon my heart lively sentiments of Faith, Hope, and Charity, with true repentance for my sins and a firm desire of amendment, while with deep affection and grief of soul I ponder within myself and mentally contemplate your five most precious wounds; having before my eyes that which David spoke in prophecy of you, O good Jesus: "They have pierced my hands and my feet; they have numbered all my bones."

—PRAYER BEFORE A CRUCIFIX

*H*e who has learned to pray

has learned the greatest secret of a

holy and happy life.

—WILLIAM LAW

*W*e beg you, Lord, to help and defend us. Deliver the oppressed, have compassion on the despised, raise the fallen, reveal yourself to the needy, heal the sick, bring back those who have strayed from you, feed the hungry, lift up the weak, remove the prisoner's chains. May every nation come to know that you are God alone, that Jesus is your Son, that we are your people, the sheep of your pasture.

—CLEMENT OF ROME

O God, through whom every good
   thing has its beginning,
and through whom it is improved and
   increased;
grant, we beseech Thee,
to us who cry to Thee,
that this work,
which we are beginning
for the praise of Thy name,
may be happily brought to completion
through the never-failing gift
of Thy fatherly wisdom.
Through Christ our Lord.
Amen.

—ANCIENT COLLECT

May God give you . . . for every storm a rainbow, for every tear a smile, for every care a promise and a blessing in each trial. For every problem life sends, a faithful friend to share, for every sigh a sweet song and an answer for each prayer.

—IRISH BLESSING

O consuming fire, Spirit of love,

descend within me and reproduce in me,

as it were, an incarnation of the Word,

that I may be to him another humanity

wherein he renews his mystery.

—ELIZABETH OF SCHONAU

*T*ake my life and let it be

Consecrated, Lord, to Thee.

Take my moments and my days—

Let them flow in ceaseless praise. . . .

Take my hands, and let them move

At the impulse of Thy love;

Take my feet, and let them be

Swift and beautiful for Thee. . . .

Take my voice and let me sing

Always, only, for my King;

Take my lips and let them be

Filled with messages from Thee. . . .

Take my silver and my gold—

Not a mite would I withhold.

Take my intellect and use

Every power as Thou shalt choose.

Take my will, and make it Thine—

It shall be no longer mine;

Take my heart—it is Thine own,

It shall be Thy royal throne. . . .

Take my love—my Lord, I pour

At Thy feet its treasure store.

Take myself—and I will be

Ever, only, all for Thee.

—FRANCES RIDLEY HAVERGAL

How sweet the name of Jesus
sounds
In a believer's ear!
It soothes his sorrows, heals his wounds,
And drives away his fear.

It makes the wounded spirit whole
And calms the troubled breast;
'Tis manna to the hungry soul,
And to the weary, rest.

Dear name! the rock on which I build

My shield and hiding place;

My never-failing treasure, filled

With boundless stores of grace!

Jesus, my Shepherd, Brother, Friend,

My Prophet, Priest, and King,

My Lord, my Life, my Way, my End,

Accept the praise I bring.

—JOHN NEWTON

*N*o prayer of adoration will ever soar higher than the simple cry: "I love you God."

—LOUIS CASSELS

*A*lmighty and eternal God, the disposer of all the affairs of the world, there is not one circumstance so great as not to be subject to Thy power, nor so small but it comes within Thy care; Thy goodness and wisdom show themselves through all Thy words, and Thy lovingkindness and mercy appear in the several dispensations of Thy providence. May we readily submit ourselves to Thy pleasure and sincerely resign our will to Thine, with all patience, meekness, and humility.

—QUEEN ANNE

*L*ead, kindly Light, amid the

encircling gloom,

Lead Thou me on;

The night is dark, and I am far

from home,

Lead Thou me on;

Keep Thou my feet. I do not ask to see

The distant scene, one step's enough

for me.

—JOHN HENRY NEWMAN

*G*od, who touches earth with beauty,

Make my heart anew;

With Thy Spirit recreate me,

Pure and strong and true.

Like Thy springs and running waters

Make me crystal pure;

Like Thy rocks of towering grandeur,

Make me strong and sure.

Like the dancing waves in sunlight,

Make me glad and free;

Like the straightness of the pine trees,

Let me upright be.

—MARY S. EDGAR

No man is greater than his prayer life.

—LEONARD RAVENHILL

The welcome of the Father's arms be
  yours
The welcome of the Savior's heart be yours
The welcome of the Spirit's call be yours.

Deep peace of this earth to you
Deep peace of this sky to you
Deep peace of this place to you.

The kindly eye of the Three be upon you
To aid and guard you
To cherish and enrich you.

May God take you in the clasp of His own
  two hands.

—CELTIC BLESSING

*H*oly Spirit, think through me till your ideas are my ideas.

—AMY CARMICHAEL

May he support us all the day long

till the shadows lengthen

and the evening comes

and the busy world is hushed

and the fever of life is over

and all our work is done

then in his mercy

may he give us a safe lodging

and a holy rest

at the last.

—JOHN HENRY NEWMAN

*I*f a man wants God to hear his prayer quickly, then before he prays for anything else, even his own soul, when he stands and stretches out his hands toward God, he must pray with all his heart for his enemies. Through this action God will hear everything that he asks.

—ZENO, DESERT FATHER

God, you have prepared in peace the path I must follow today. Help me to walk straight on that path. If I speak, remove lies from my lips. If I am hungry, take away from me all complaint. If I have plenty, destroy pride in me. May I go through the day calling on you, O Lord, you who know no other Lord.

—ETHIOPIAN PRAYER

*M*aker of all things, God most high,

Great ruler of the starry sky,

Who, robing day with beauteous light,

Hast clothes in soft repose the night,

That sleep may wearied limbs restore,

And fit for toil and use once more,

May gently soothe the careworn breast,

And lull our anxious griefs to rest.

We thank thee for the day that's gone;

We pray thee for the night come on;

O help us sinners as we raise

To thee our votive hymn of praise.

From every carnal passion free

O may our hearts repose in thee!

Nor envious fiend, with harmful snare,

Our rest with sinful terrors share.

Christ with the Father ever one,

Spirit! The Father and the Son,

God over all, the mighty sway,

Shield us, great Trinity, we pray.

—AMBROSE OF MILAN

*L*ord, heal me, and I will truly be

healed. Save me, and I will truly be saved.

—JEREMIAH THE PROPHET,
JEREMIAH 17:14 (NCV)

*L*ord, I rejoice

 that nothing

 can come between me and your love,

 even when I feel alone or in difficulty,

 when in sickness or am troubled.

Even if attacked or afraid,

 no abyss of mine is so deep

 that your love is not deeper still.

Lord,

 you have experienced many hells of

 this world but descended so that you

 can lift us up.

Be always near.

—CORRIE TEN BOOM

*T*ake thy first walk with God!

Let Him go forth with thee; by

stream, or sea, or mountain path,

seek still His company.

—HORATIUS BONAR

This day, Lord, may I dream

  your dreams,

this day, Lord, may I reflect your love,

this day, Lord, may I do your work,

this day, may I taste your peace.

—ANGELA ASHWIN

*W*e thank thee, O God, for the spiritual nature of man. We are in nature but we live above nature.

Help us never to let anybody or any condition pull us so low as to cause us to hate. Give us strength to love our enemies and to do good to those who despitefully use us and persecute us. We thank thee for thy Church, founded upon thy Word, that challenges us to do more than sing and pray, but go out and work as though the very answer to our prayers depended on us and not upon thee. Then, finally, help us to realize that man was created to shine like stars and live on through all eternity. Keep us, we pray, in perfect peace; help us to walk together, pray together, sing together, and live together until that day when all God's children, Black, White, Red, and Yellow will rejoice in one common bond of humanity in the kingdom of our Lord and of our God, we pray. Amen.

—MARTIN LUTHER KING JR.

𝒯hank You for this time of quiet with You in which I can receive the peace of knowing that I am loved and forgiven, the healing of the hurts of harbored memories, the answers to problems that often seem unsolvable and the vision for solutions that otherwise would be beyond my human understanding.

—LLOYD JOHN OGILVIE

*T*ime spent in prayer is never

wasted.

—FRANÇOIS DE FÉNELON

*L*ord, Jesus,
I sign my heart with the sign of the cross,
reminding myself
of your love for each person.
I ask that I may grow in faithfulness
as your friend.

I sign my lips with the sign of the cross,
that I may speak as you would speak.

I sign my hands with the sign of the cross
asking that you would enable me
to do your work, and be your hands
in our world which you love so much.

I sign my eyes with the sign of your cross
that I may really see, Lord,
and be aware of all that is around me.

I sign my ears with the sign of your cross
That I may listen and really hear

The communication that comes to me
In different ways
—from you
and from the people
you place into my life.

I sign my shoulders, Lord, with your cross,
knowing that you call me
to carry my own cross each day
and support others
in the burdens and difficulties
that they have.

All that I do today
I set out to do
in the name of the Father
and of the Son
and of the Holy Spirit. Amen.

—SIGNING WITH THE CROSS,
JESUIT PRAYER

O Lord, God, from whom we come,

in whom we are enfolded, to whom we

shall return:

Bring us in our pilgrimage through life;

With the power of the Father protecting,

With the love of Jesus indwelling,

And the light of the Spirit guiding,

Until we come to our ending,

In life and love eternal.

—PETER NOTT

*D*o not pray for easy lives.

Pray to be stronger men. Do not

pray for tasks equal to your powers.

Pray for power equal to your tasks.

—PHILLIPS BROOKS

Lord, when we have not any light,

And mothers are asleep,

Then through the stillness of the night

Your little children keep.

When shadows haunt the quiet room,

Help us to understand

That you are with us through

   the gloom,

To hold us by the hand.

—ANNIE MATHESON

*T*hou hast given so much to me,

Give one thing more—a grateful heart;

Not thankful when it pleaseth me,

As if Thy blessings had spare days,

But such a heart whose pulse may be

Thy praise.

—GEORGE HERBERT

O what peace we often forfeit,

O what needless pain we bear,

All because we do not carry

Everything to God in prayer.

—JOSEPH M. SCRIVEN

ABOUT THE EDITOR

Jim Palmer is founding pastor of the
Pilgrimage Project in Nashville,
Tennessee, where he and his family
reside. He actively mentors others in
cultivating an intimate relationship
with God through prayer.